C000004781

How to Flirt with Women

*The Art of Flirting
Without Being Creepy That
Turns Her On!
How to Approach, Talk to &
Attract Women
(Dating Advice for Men)*

Ray Asher

© **Copyright 2020 Ray Asher**

- All rights reserved.

This content is provided with the sole purpose of providing relevant information on a specific topic for which every reasonable effort has been made to ensure that it is both accurate and reasonable. Nevertheless, by purchasing this content you consent to the fact that the author, as well as the publisher, are in no way experts on the topics contained herein, regardless of any claims as such that may be made within. As such, any suggestions or recommendations that are made within are done so purely for entertainment value. It is recommended that you always consult a professional prior to undertaking any of the advice or techniques discussed within.

This is a legally binding declaration that is considered both valid and fair by both the Committee of Publishers Association and the American Bar Association and should be considered as legally binding within the United States.

The reproduction, transmission, and duplication of any of the content found herein, including any specific or extended information will be done as an illegal act regardless of the end form the information ultimately takes. This includes copied versions of the work both physical, digital and audio unless express consent of the Publisher is provided beforehand. Any additional rights reserved.

Furthermore, the information that can be found within the pages described forthwith shall be considered both accurate and truthful when it comes to the recounting of facts. As such, any use, correct or incorrect, of the provided information will render the Publisher free of responsibility as to the actions taken outside of their direct purview. Regardless, there are zero scenarios where the original author or the Publisher can be deemed liable in any fashion for any damages or hardships that may result from any of the information discussed herein.

Additionally, the information in the following pages is intended only for informational purposes and should thus be thought of as universal. As befitting its nature, it is presented without assurance regarding its prolonged validity or interim quality. Trademarks that are mentioned are done without written consent and can in no way be considered an endorsement from the trademark holder.

Table of Content

Your Free Resource Is Awaiting

To better help you, I've created a simple mind map you can use _right away_ to easily understand, quickly recall and readily use what you'll be learning in this book.

Click Here To Get Your Free Resource

Alternatively, here's the link:

https://viebooks.club/freeresourcemind-mapforhowtoflirtwithwomen

Your Free Resource Is Waiting..

Get Your Free Resource Now!

Introduction

You picked up this book for a specific purpose. Something is missing in your life.

You want to learn how to meet and flirt with women. You want to learn how to easily talk, joke and laugh with them and have them return the flirtation. Just like all men, you want to be able to have a connection with a woman and enjoy it as the conversation deepens and becomes more intimate.

It's not that difficult, and I am going to show you how to do it! And not just flirt. I'm going to show you how to listen, respond, joke and touch women in a way where you don't come off as a creep or violate their space.

But before we get started, you probably want to know why I am telling you all of this and how I gained this knowledge.

As a young man, I was pretty introverted. I would talk to girls in high school but often was ignored. Women didn't take any interest in me. I didn't know how to open up a conversation or how to keep their interest. Often, my interest was ignored.

High school was horrible. A quick side note to any of my readers who are currently in high school or just finished: high school is tough for everybody. The person who said that your high school years are the best of your life must have died the day after their graduation. Believe me, it gets better. You have your whole life in front of you.

After I got out of high school, I left for college, which was thousands of miles away from where I grew up. I left behind bad memories and experiences and arrived on campus ready to explore a whole new world.

Quickly, I fell into my old habits of jokes that made others roll their eyes and nervous banter. But in my new environment, I realized that I wasn't dealing with high school girls running to class with a giggle about the latest pop star. These were a new group of women, those who were driven, ready to take on the world and build a career, and they were more serious in the kind of man that they want to be with.

Now I was dealing with women. The rules had changed, so I needed to change.

I learned a lot in college about how to talk, flirt and listen to women, how to have conversations that led to dates and more. By the time I graduated, I was a completely different person—assured, flirtatious and ready to have a great time.

But it took a few years in the real world as I started working and began to interact with more women of all ages. As I met and flirted with them, some of what I had learned in college still worked, but this was different. So, I tried different things, I practiced and saw what worked. I also saw what didn't work.

And now I can flirt with any woman in the world. But it's not some superpower. It's not some amazing thing that only I know how to do. It's just about confidence, listening and observing.

Part One: Flirting Fundamentals

Chapter 1: Flirting

What is Flirting?

It seems pretty simple, but let's break it down.

Flirting is simply letting someone know that you have an interest in them through talking, writing or non-verbal cues. It can be playful with no real intended outcome or for specific purposes like getting a date or hooking up.

Throughout history, people around the world have used many different ways to flirt. In some cultures, a kiss was simply a form of flirtation, where in other societies it is only allowed for involved couples. In the past, Europeans did all their flirting with the simple use of fans and hand signals. At one point in Japan, it was all done with the eyes and no talking.

So, you can already see that there is no perfect, one-size-fits-all way to flirt with women. It's different by country, culture and, quite honestly, by person. This is one of the major reasons that having a go-to pick-up line or hook may work from time to time but, in the long run, is a failing way of trying to meet women. So, if you have been reading books or articles claiming they have the "only way" to meet women, it's not true. You need to use the tools you have as well as some tweaks to find the approach that is genuine to who you are.

Flirting is just about finding a way to close the gap between two people. Some people flirt normally, it's just a part of their personality, and sometimes they don't even realize they are doing it. It's how they often get their way, and it's just part of their personality.

For others, it can be a bit more difficult, and they might need some help to get things started.

If you are interested in someone, you want to close that gap not just physically but psychologically. Flirting gives you a way to test the waters and move closer.

I hear people say all the time that they don't know how to flirt or that they just can't do it. That is not true! Anybody can flirt. In fact, even if you say you don't know how, you probably do, you just didn't realize it.

What's Your Goal?

You want her to want to keep talking to you. It's how you are going to get her phone number or however the evening may progress.

Now, if your goal is to have sex, that's fine, but it can't be at the forefront of your mind when you approach a woman and flirt with her. She's going to be able to tell because you are not in the moment with her, you are thinking about something that may or may not happen. It especially isn't going to happen once she realizes that's all that is on your mind.

Flirting can also just brighten your and someone else's day. Try it sometime. A friendly smile and some easy banter can make a big difference in how someone's day goes. That's not to say that women—or men, for that matter—want to be hit on all the time, but a little kindness, flattery and playfulness can go a long way to lifting someone's spirits.

Types of Flirting

You may not believe it, but even scientists have gotten into the act and broken-down flirting. A study at the University of Kansas using nearly 10,000 people studied how they flirt and divided them into five categories [1]:

Traditional Flirting

Good old-fashioned flirting. Jokes, winks, smiles and clever words in order to make a connection with the other person and move toward a larger conversation or date.

Physical

This is the simple physical flirting. Touching a knee or arm, but not in an overly sexual or un-comfortable way. It's about making that physical connection.

Sincere

When you pay a compliment or comment on something that you really believe. It's about find-ing common ground and sharing with the other person. It might be about clothing or something they are doing, but it's always genuine.

Playful

Playful flirting is more about enjoying the act of flirting. Some people don't even realize they are doing it. It's just sort of woven into their personality. You've met girls like this who talk flirtatiously to everyone, often to get their own way. It's not always a bad thing, but it can be used in manipulative ways.

Polite

Sometimes this isn't even seen as flirting. By being nice, it's actually a way of introducing yourself and who you are. But be careful. If it's too subtle, they won't even realize you are doing it and might not pay attention to you. When you want to gain someone's attention, you want to be bold enough to really get them to notice, not so subtle that they don't even notice what you are doing.

Why Does Flirting Work?

Flirting works because everyone wants to make a connection. Even if someone isn't going to go home with you that night, it doesn't mean that they don't enjoy some good old-fashioned flirting.

The truth is we all flirt in our everyday life, even if it's just a smile. It doesn't have to be romantic; it can be for other purposes.

Have you ever smiled at a barista in order to get an extra shot of espresso? Or complimented someone at the DMV hoping they could help you out with a small problem? Well, guess what? You've been flirting.

Women have been doing it since the dawn of man. How many girls do you know who have gotten out of a traffic ticket with a wink and sexy smile?

It works because everybody wants to have that warm feeling when a connection is made. And nowhere is this more relevant than when you are talking to a beautiful woman.

Flirting is how we let someone know we are interested in them. It's the primer for the sexual fire. Those moments of wonder, getting to know someone, the lure of the stranger who is interested, it gets the hormones and pheromones going.

That's what all of this is about, stoking that fire with flirtation.

Why Do Most Men Suck at Flirting?

A recent university study paired up 52 couples of men and women and asked them to talk to each other. Afterwards, the individuals were questioned about their experiences and how they interacted with their partner [2].

One interesting thing that comes up is that many women don't even realize when a man has been flirting with them. There are a number of reasons for this. Maybe the woman of interest was too preoccupied with something at work. Maybe they weren't good at recognizing when the flirting was going on. Or maybe the man was so subtle, the flirting was hard to see.

So, why are men so bad at flirting?

Part of it is fear. Men will keep their flirting extremely low-key and subtle because they don't want to be embarrassed. The woman might not respond the way they hoped or call them out and embarrass them.

There's a safety zone to flirting very subtly because if it doesn't work, it can easily just be said to be a friendly joke.

It's also because they don't listen and change their game plan as they get more information. All too often, men approach a woman with a specific approach, and when it doesn't work, they freeze. They aren't confident enough in themselves to change their direction and go with the conversational flow. They think they only have one or two things they can do or say when, in reality, they have near limitless options!

Why Is It Important to Flirt?

First and foremost, it's how you get to know a woman. It's how you can break down the initial walls and discover them as a person and build the groundwork for getting her number, going on a date and beyond.

When someone flirts, it's a chance to see inside the workings of their mind and experience how they interact and what they are into. That's why it's so important to be observant. She is literally giving you all the clues you need to get to know her, impress her and sweep her off her feet!

Plus, it's fun! Who doesn't like to give and get attention?

You are also building anticipation. You may or may not end up sleeping with this woman, but the game of flirting is creating a buildup. It's about the thrill of the hunt.

The Art of Seduction

Seduction is merely presenting an energy that makes the person you are talking to comfortable and bringing that connection closer and closer. It's about psychology.

People respond to energy that is expended for them. We usually say seduction is flowers, wine, and a romantic dinner. That can be part of it, but it's much more.

It's about creating an environment through your actions and words that makes a woman feel safe and important at the same time. At that moment, there is no one else in the world as central as she is to you and she will reciprocate.

There are a number of important points to seduction if it is to work properly:

Presentation

You need to present yourself as a catch. For her to completely fall into the seduction conversation, she needs to believe you are worth her time, mind and body.

Listening

It serves several purposes. Not only are you getting to know her to see if you want to pursue this woman, but it also builds her confidence in you because you are hearing what she is saying.

Plus, it provides you with a list of things to discuss, pursue and joke about. The more you learn about her, the more ammunition you have. Don't continue with a certain line of questioning if you learn new information about her. Not only does it open opportunities, but it also shows that you are actually involved in the conversation by pushing it forward.

Safety

In order for a woman to "let herself go" physically and emotionally, she needs to feel a certain degree of safety. Not just that you aren't going to kidnap her or do something horrible, but that you aren't going to hurt her emotionally.

Your words, actions and even your presence need to create a safe space where she can open up to you and let herself be a bit vulnerable. This is true when you first meet, your first date and even into a relationship. Trust is very important.

Slow. Slow. Slow.

Seduction is a bit like a relationship, albeit on a much smaller scale. It's about anticipation.

For a woman to feel seduced in a good way, it needs to feel like it's moving through stages. Women don't want to feel like they've raced through a one-night stand or date. They want to enjoy it and feel like they are going through a process. They want the romance, the feeling of effort in an effortless situation.

Chapter 2: How Women Look at Flirting

Men and women are wired differently. It's just a biological fact.

On a primal level, men are looking for certain things, while women are searching for something different.

Since the early days of human society, women have searched for things in potential partners that will check off specific boxes on their inner checklist. Protector, reproduction and provider. It's on a base level, and that's what shapes their attraction and what flirting they will respond to.

How a Woman's Mind and Body Works When It Comes to Romance

Contrary to popular belief, not every woman is romantic. But most are.

Many have what could be considered more masculine qualities or are more logical in their approach to romance, but the truth is the majority of women, no matter how closed-off or tough they might be on the outside, still have a romantic side that they want to be fulfilled.

A romantic woman wants to experience the world with her man. She wants to have a partner who protects her but at the same time shares experiences with her.

Women want surprises and mystery. They want their man to show them they care and are interested.

How Women Flirt

When it comes to flirting, women are going to give out a lot of signs to show they are interested. On their own, these signs might not seem very important. If a woman does just one of these things, it doesn't mean that they are flirting. But if you are paying attention and notice that a few of these signs show up, then you know she is interested in you.

First, look for the eye contact. With women, the talking is in the eyes. If you are having a conversation with her and you notice that she is ogling you from head to toe, this is a good sign that you have made an impression, and she is interested.

Next, look for a smile. The smile can be a hard one. Some women will smile to be friendly or to be polite, but if the smile goes from one ear to the other and it doesn't go away, then they are most likely flirting with you.

Another thing to consider is whether or not they touch you. Women who have no interest in the person they are talking to will keep those hands still and most likely near their sides. But if you notice that they are lightly touching your arm, grazing up against you, or letting your legs touch when sitting down, it is definitely a good sign.

Women also tend to draw attention to more private parts of their bodies while flirting. No, not *those* private parts. Ones that are legal to show in public. Has she brushed her hair aside and left her neck exposed? Does she keep running her fingers over the inner part of her wrist? If yes, she might just be flirting. Such movements are meant to draw your eye to parts of her body not typically exposed during conversation. It's an attempt to show a small level of vulnerability and trust beyond the norm, which means that she might be trying to let you know that she's open to something more intimate than conversation.

You can also look at the hair. When a woman is flirting, perhaps because they are nervous, they are more likely to twirl their hair. This is more of an unconscious habit that means that they are either curious about you or open to your advances.

Many women will show their interest by trying to have lively banter and laughing at your jokes. Listen to the laugh. If it is actually genuine, they aren't being polite. They like you and enjoy the things that you are saying, even if you know that your jokes aren't funny.

Finally, another thing to look for is the direction that she is facing. If a woman is not that interested, they might face out and away from you, like they are ready to leave. When they focus their body and their energy to you, this is a signal that they are open and interested. Look at their feet and see which position they are pointing. This will help you to determine whether there is some interest there or not.

What Makes Men Attractive to Women?

Beyond personal taste, some universals appeal to women. Obviously, some women like tall men, some like short, some like muscular while others like lean. Some women swoon for dark hair, while others like certain skin tones. For some of these things, there isn't anything you can do about this, but there are other things that you can do that will make you more appealing to women across the board.

I've penned an entire book about the subject, ***How to Attract Women***. I would urge you to check it out for a complete take on how you can be more attractive to the opposite sex.

Here are some basic things women look for in a potential mate:

Security

They want to know you are there for them. It doesn't mean that you are going to be their caveman and protect them from wild animals. It means that they can trust you and be secure with you that you won't hurt them (mentally or physically) or cheat on them.

Chemistry

This is a simple one. They want sparks. They want the butterflies in their stomach when they see you and the electricity between you when you stroke her hair.

Many people think that chemistry just happens or it doesn't. It is very true that there can be immediate chemistry from almost the first time you lock eyes. However, other times you might need to help the chemistry along. Don't let this be your excuse to constantly bug and harass the woman. But sometimes, some carefully placed flirting over a few weeks or so can help the woman open up to your advances. If you try to open up with them and they keep turning you down, then it is time to move on.

Permanence

They want to know that you have your life together or at least have plans. This also applies to your relationship. They don't want drama and a rocky relationship. They want you to be their rock.

Permanence could also be a simple as just knowing that you aren't a player. They might just want to know that you are in the moment with them and haven't been working your way around the bar and already have a booty call lined up for later. Permanence to a woman can just mean that you are only interested in her right now.

Equals

A woman wants you to treat her as an equal. Long gone are the days when the status quo was a woman who stayed home waiting with a man's slippers and drink. They want to know you respect them and will support them in whatever their goals might be.

It can be conversation, insight or just a respect for her thoughts and ideals. Plus, flirting and having a conversation with someone you consider (and is) on the same level as you are much more fun, fulfilling and, in all honesty, will move forward much quicker.

Passion

Women love passion, and it's not just about the bedroom. Women love that you are passionate about things. Not just her, but your work, your family, your goals and even your hobbies, as long as they don't entirely dominate your life. Women will support this and find it sexy.

Intelligence

Showing off the different sides to your intelligence can really help you to impress a woman. Getting to know her will make a difference in how well you are received by her. Some women are interested in a man who can change a tire and fix up something in a home. Other women may be more interested in someone who can recite Shakespeare and impress their friends at social events. Learning which parts of your intelligence are the most important to that particular woman will make a difference.

Creativity

Just like there are different kinds of intelligence, there are also different kinds of creativity. Creativity can be writing, painting, sculpting, acting, decorating a home and all the other "traditional" displays of the word. But it can also include thinking on your feet, finding out-of-the-box solutions and being able to come up with acceptable compromises in heated disagreements. They all show that a man can think in unique ways and find the not-so-obvious answers, something crucial for survival. Different women will be impressed by different kinds of creativity, and many women will be impressed by multiple kinds. Like with intelligence, it just takes getting to know the woman first.

Confidence

Confidence can be perceived as an overall level of comfort and security while interacting with women. Thus, you appear to be in control of your emotions and your ability to communicate. Furthermore, you don't appear to be anxious or desperate to somehow connect.

Women love this. There is nothing sexier than confidence. However, don't spill over into cockiness or overconfidence. This is a killer.

Confidence is such an important part of interacting with women, you are going to see me come back to it again and again, across my books.

Is She Flirting Back?

You can flirt all you want, but if you don't know if it's working, it isn't exactly any use, is it?

Look for the signs that she's into you or flirting back.

- **Look for the sideways glance.** She's going to try to get a look at you when she doesn't think you notice. Keep an eye out for that glance over when she's sipping her drink or if she is walking away from you.

- **The hair toss.** It's been joked about for years, but that's because it's true. The hair flip is an age-old sign that she's interested. Also, watch for when she twists or plays with it.

- **A genuine smile.** A genuine smile changes and it's hard to get rid of, sort of like getting the giggles. In contrast to a "defensive smile", which can appear plastered and be turned on and off like a switch.

- **Leaning into you.** When anyone, not just women, is interested in a conversation and the person, they tend to lean forward without even knowing it.

- **Touch.** If she touches your arm or leg, it means she's interested in you. Any physical connection (other than a right hook to the jaw) is a great sign. Even if it's while laughing or leaning on you to fix an article of clothing or adjust her shoe. If she likes you, she's going to find reasons to touch you.

- **Engagement.** Look for her nodding her head as you talk or laughing and reacting at the right spots. This means she is really into what you are saying and the person who is saying it.

- **Body language.** Are her legs turned away from you? Or are her arms folded across her chest and leaning away? These are defensive positions, and they're signs she's being polite but not that into you. If her body language is more open and she is turned toward you, it's a sign that she's interested.

- **Whispering in your ear.** Unless she's telling you to go away, this is always a good sign.

- **Legitimate compliments.** In some cases, women are going to show you that she is interested by giving you a lot of compliments. Take a look at this and see what kinds of things she is complimenting you on, if she is going out of her way to compliment you and whether she is doing it to flirt or just to show her interest.

Is She Flirting or Just Friendly?

Sometimes it's difficult to tell if the woman you are talking with is flirting back or just a really friendly person. I will admit, there are times I've even fallen into this trap. But if you handle the situation right and look for the signs, you'll be able to figure it out.

- **Pay attention to the eye contact.** If it is intense and lasts a long time, odds are she's flirting with you and not just being friendly.

- **Physical contact.** The more she touches you, the more you know it's not just a pleasant conversation.

- **How the conversation goes matters.** If she turns the conversation toward other topics about you, your life and deeper things, then she's moving from friend to flirting, especially if it turns toward the subject of sex.

- **Look for the cues when she isn't talking.** Not just touching, but playful motions like touching her hair, her lips, adjusting clothing or even just being a bit fidgety can be signs of flirting and excitement.

- **She makes it very clear she's single.** She wants to make sure you know that she's in play. It's like when a girl makes it known she has a boyfriend, she wants that information out there.

- **She teases you.** This one is a bit tough because it can go either way early in a conversation and flirting. If she's not into you, she might tease as a defense mechanism. Or it might be a way to get closer to the real you. Experience will help you learn, but you may have a few false starts. Don't let it get you down.

- **Look at her feet.** Seriously. Are they pointed away from you or toward you? People will naturally turn toward someone they are interested in talking to. If her feet are pointing toward you, this is a signal her body is. If they are pointing away from you, her body language is closed off, and you may not be doing too well.

Tests That She Will Give You

So, that's it? You just be charming, listen and women will flirt, and it's all golden, right?

Not so much. Women are going to test you. They might be seeing if they want to date you, or it might be just if they are going to sleep with you or even just kiss you. So, there are different tests that they will secretly give you, and you probably don't even know it.

Every woman is different, and some are actually testing you subconsciously, not completely aware they are doing it. If you are mindful, you can keep an eye out for these tests and not only pass them but use them to see if the woman you are interested in is worth your time.

The "In the Moment" Test

A woman wants to know that you are there with them, physically and mentally. If you are concentrating on work, the sports score, your texts or social media, she's not going to be impressed. If you are only thinking about how to get her into bed, she's going to figure it out.

She wants a man who gives her the attention she feels she deserves and is present in the moment with her. So, give her your attention and listen. Respond and ask questions because with this test, she is absolutely right.

The Courage Test

I was talking with a woman once who said I was big enough to beat up any guy in the bar. Now, truthfully, while I have been in my fair share of fights, I'm not a big fan of violence. I can and will defend myself and have on a number of occasions, but I'm not one who goes looking for a fight.

But this woman decided to try to pick a fight with another guy in the bar and have me come to her rescue by saying I would beat the guy up. I was lucky because the guy looked at me and backed down, but I also knew I was done with that woman.

She was trying to give me the Courage Test but doing it in a way that showed me her true intentions. She was trying to manipulate me to see if I would protect her but also do what she wanted. And I don't play that game.

However, there are other times the Courage Test is given, and usually, when it's done organically, it's a big win for you. If an event comes up where you can truly show your courage or bravery- a real fight, pulling her out of danger or even just killing a spider that she's afraid of- it'll go a long way to pass her test. Plus, she'll know it's legitimate because you acted instinctively versus her trying to set you up.

The Thoughtful Test

Women want a man who is thinking of them but not dependent on their attention. So, they will often test you on your thoughtfulness or how well you remember and react to certain things. Small gestures go a long way. Remembering events or rough days can make a real impression. Contrary to what most people think, a woman will be far more affected by a meaningful gift or a truthful and well-meaning comment than a flashy dinner or car or gifts.

Something I will do is pay attention to what they are drinking. It doesn't matter if it's at a bar, a restaurant or coffee shop. Does she put ice in her drink? Does she like a twist of lime in her drink? Or extra cream in her coffee? I watch for this and file it away.

Then when the next opportunity arises, either to get refills or the next time I see her, I'll offer to get her a drink and use the information I have. I'll never assume, I'll always ask. This proves three things to her- I listen, I'm thoughtful, and I'm not presumptuous.

The Good Man Test

I hear it all the time. "Men are dogs." Now, I do not deny that a lot of them are, but there are a few good men out there. Ones that won't cheat, ones that treat women well. But the majority of women have run into so many guys who act like boys that they begin to assume that's the way all men are.

So, she is going to test you to try to find out if you are hiding anything. She's going to ask questions about your life (often in coded ways) to learn if you like to go out with the boys, go to bars, have had a lot of girlfriends or go on a lot of dates.

Now is not the time to tell her stories of one-night stands and drunken nights out with your buddies. Let her know that you like to have fun, but you know there is not only a time and place but a proper way to behave.

The Jealousy Test

This is another test that will tell you a lot about the woman you are interested in. Some women like the drama that comes from men being jealous and the thrill of fighting over her (see my above story about my experience with the Courage Test). Personally, I think these women are a waste of time and energy, and while they may be fun to talk to for a few minutes, in the end, it's going to turn into a nightmare.

These are the women who will tell you how some-one else was flirting with them in order to get a rise out of you. You may think it would be fun to take them home for a great evening of sex, but I caution you that the next morning or the next time they see you, this woman is going to be clingy and manipulative. These are women who thrive on drama.

There are some women though who use this test properly. They don't want a jealous man, so they just want to see if you react. It's more about seeing that you are mature and can handle an adult interaction. So, make sure you know exactly what her motives are before you decide to walk away.

The Patience Test

Some women want to see how serious you are. It might be long term, like not returning texts or calls, or it could just be in the bar she makes you wait through the evening to see if you keep coming back.

This one can be difficult. You want to show you have interest, but at the same time, you don't want to come across as desperate. In the flirtation realm, always be happy to talk with her but never chase her.

The Tease Test

This is a test some women will use to see how thick your skin might be. They'll tease you about a subject to gauge how you react. Do you tease back, or do you get offended and fly off the handle? Or can you take a joke?

This tells them how sensitive you are, but it also can tell you a bit about them. Depending on how they tease, you can see deeper into their actual personality. Are they light-hearted or does the teasing become cruel and demeaning? This can be a sign of a woman trying to make a power play. It could be a sign of her personality or a sign of her just toying with you before she gives you the brush-off. Or she could just be an unpleasantly sarcastic woman.

The Free Time Test

Eventually, the conversation may turn toward your hobbies and what you do in your free time. What you answer is going to shape how she sees you. If you tell her that you collect comic books, she may automatically picture you as living in your parent's basement. But if you tell her that you like to spend time in nature, climbing, and hiking, she's going to see you differently. This doesn't mean that you should lie about what you do, but maybe consider a different way of explaining it. Telling the girl that you like to collect comic books may not give her the picture that you want. Instead, highlight some of the positive things you like to do.

Make sure that your free time sounds exciting and something she thinks is interesting. The more she thinks it would be fun to join you, the quicker you will pass this test!

The Lie Detector Test

Women hate liars. Scratch that—*everyone* hates liars. So, naturally, there might come a time when the woman you're flirting with decides to test your honesty. Try not to take this personally. More than anything else, it's a self-defense mechanism built on the backs of many lying jerks that came before you.

This test is one of the harder ones to recognize as it slips so easily into any conversation. Essentially, she will find a point in the conversation where she can naturally slip in a reference back to something you mentioned earlier but with a twist. If you don't correct the discrepancy, either through gentle but direct correction or by subtly fixing the detail in your response, then she will take notice and continue your conversation more guarded than before. She might even find a way to get away from you entirely if she deems the incident a big enough offense.

This test can tell you a lot about both the woman you're flirting with and yourself. If she gives you this test at all, she's probably had problems with liars in the past. She might also have trust issues.

Chapter 3: The Mindset of Flirting and the Core Principals

So, how can you be successful at flirting and how do you start?

The Core Principals of Flirting

There are literally millions of ways to flirt with a woman. Not just different styles like verbal and non-verbal, joking, telling stories and teasing and so much more, but because every man, woman, and situation was different. What works for you may not work for someone else.

That's one of the things that always excites me about starting up a conversation with a woman. I never know what she will be like or how it will go.

I can feel my adrenaline pumping even after all this time. It never gets old!

There are definitely core principals and rules that you need to adhere to in order to be successful in flirting with women.

The Mindset

You have to have a certain mindset as you flirt. By being in the right place in your head, you will react differently, be in the moment and be successful.

Abundance

The first part of a successful flirting mindset is believing in abundance.

All that means is that you realize that there is an endless number of women out there and there is no reason that you can't be successful with all of them!

Think of it like this. When you go out on a job interview, do you think that there's no way you'll get it, you might as well stay home and why even bother? Of course you don't!

You go into that interview with your best foot forward, proud of your accomplishments and ready to be the best person for the job. You are positive and confident. Of course they want to hire you!

It's the same with women! You have to have the mindset that any woman you talk to is going to be interested in you. It's not about arrogance; it's just about realizing you have an abundance of opportunities. Your confidence will skyrocket, and you will see successes you never imagined.

Keep it Lighthearted

Flirting is like playing. You can't get too serious or offended. If she says something that sounds like she's shutting you down, it's ok. Just shake it off. If she tells you she's not interested, it's all good. What did you lose?

It's Fun

You should be enjoying this. It's fun. You are talking with a beautiful woman and making her laugh, smile and start to fall for you!

Be in the moment. Enjoy what you are doing and relax. It's just a conversation, and you're going to be fine.

Never Be Cocky

Don't be full of yourself. We've all made jokes about the cologne-wearing guy with the silk shirt and chains who believes he is God's gift to women. He sidles up to them at the bar, throws out a line and adjusts his toupee but then blames the woman when she brushes him off.

Don't be this guy. But you don't dress like that, right? How could you be that guy?

Well, you can still be overconfident and cocky even if you don't outwardly dress like it. Women can tell insincerity. Be confident but be yourself. You are a great person with a lot to offer.

How to Be Successful at Flirting

Several keys are vital to being successful at flirting. I've already mentioned some of them, but I cannot overstate how important they are.

Be Relaxed

You need to be relaxed, man. You need to act as if this is the easiest thing you've ever done. I promise you, it will become easier.

In fact, it will become second nature. There is going to be a point where you just had a flirtatious conversation with a girl, got her number and you honestly don't even remember what you did. It's like any skill. Practice until it becomes muscle memory. You won't even have to think about it.

Be Genuine

Be you, whoever that is. Now, if the real you is a boorish, loud, obnoxious, vulgar guy, you might want to revisit yourself. Sure, there are girls that like this, but if you are looking to appeal to more women (and, honestly, people in general), you might want to reconsider some of your core values and how you view the world.

Be Appropriate

Whether it's the subject matter, what you say or even touching her appropriately, be aware. Look for clues that she's responding to what you are saying. Body language can tell you if she's offended or interested.

A good rule of thumb is to avoid touch until she seems to be comfortable. Even then, a light touch on the shoulder or arm might be fine. However, it might be best to wait for her to initiate touch. If you touch her first, it might not only creep her out, but it might get you slapped with a sexual harassment complaint. So, it pays to be a little extra careful in avoiding unsolicited touching.

How Not to Come Across as a Creep

It happens to the best of us. A misunderstood line or out-of-context look and suddenly you've been labeled. You're a creep.

Sometimes it is going to be your total fault. Just accept it. I'll even admit that it still happens from time to time to me. Usually, it's a misunderstanding or something completely out of my control. It can even be something from their past you had nothing to do with.

One time, I had made some completely normal but a bit flirtatious comments to a nice woman but quickly she turned and excused herself, and that was the end of it. From her response, I knew she wasn't comfortable.

Later that evening, I happened to talk to one of her friends, and she told me that she was uncomfortable around me and felt a bit creeped out. I didn't understand because I had said nothing that could be taken as even the least bit offensive. Her friend assured me it was nothing I had done. Instead, her friend had a bad breakup with an ex, and apparently, I looked a lot like him.

There was nothing I could do about that, and I don't blame her. But it goes to show that sometimes things are going to be out of your control and a woman may not react positively. It's not your fault.

So, make sure you do everything you can to eliminate the Creep Factor.

- First and foremost: No means No. It doesn't matter if it's when you first begin to talk to her, later in the evening or if things are getting intimate. If she says no or stop, you listen immediately.

- Don't stare at her from across the room. Flash her a glance, see if she reciprocates but don't stare her down.

- Don't dwell on her appearance. Don't make constant comments about her body or certain parts. She is not going to respond the way you think. However, once you get further in your conversation, you will be able to make more sexual comments, but you need the foundation that you aren't a creep first so she will take the comments in a fun spirit.

- Don't stare or leer at certain body parts.

- Be organic in talking with her. Don't rush right to questions about relationship status or sex. Don't force your own topics on her.

- Be very careful about physical presence. Don't stand over her or corner her against a wall. Make sure she doesn't feel trapped or helpless.

- Don't just work your way around the room throwing out flirtations. Women are very observant, and she'll know.

- Don't put her up on a pedestal or make cheesy comments about her. Pickup lines are still pickup lines and, to most women, pretty dang creepy.

- Never touch a woman unless you are shaking her hand until you've reached a point in the conversation where it is proper and acceptable.

Part Two: In the Field

Chapter 4: Take a Good Look at Your Self

The way you present yourself in everyday life is just as important as the words that come out of your mouth.

So, take a good look at yourself — the entire package. You don't have to walk around in expensive suits with a Rolex and a flashy car. It's about presentation, confidence, self-esteem, and self-care.

Hygiene

It seems so simple. Basic hygiene. We all do it, right? We're not savages in the Stone Age, right?

You might be surprised what some men consider presentable and others who believe that women will respond to their dirty, shaggy and often smelly exterior.

- **Shower regularly.** You wouldn't think I need to say it, but I do. And wash EVERY-WHERE.

- **Clean and trim your nails.** Consider getting a manicure. There's nothing feminine about it. Women are going to notice, and they will respond positively.

- **Brush your teeth, floss, and mouth-wash.** Again, you wouldn't think I would need to say this. At least twice a day. Also, consider carrying some gum but be careful of medical-smelling breath sprays or mouthwash.

- **Shave the way that's right for you.** You might be the scruffy type, and that's great, but even a scruffy look requires maintenance. Shave, trim and use cream to keep scruff or your beard soft so she will want to touch and kiss you.

- **Pluck those hairs.** Nostrils, ears, and back. If you can't get to them, ask your barber or consider getting a wax job. It might hurt a bit, but it'll be worth it.

- **Use deodorant**. No matter what celebrities might say about going au natural in the deodorant department, don't do it. And don't use one of those heavy-style body sprays as deodorant.

- **Be wary of cologne.** You may think it makes you smell manly, but the girl your talking to may see it as a warning signal or maybe be offended by the smell. So, use it sparingly. Test it on some plutonic female friends for their opinions.

- **Take care of your skin**. Keep it clean and moisturized.

- **Wash your face.** If you are younger and dealing with acne, wash your face regularly and use medication to clear up any breakouts. It's not just young men, either; I still get pimples from time to time and have to laugh about it. Try special adult care creams to get rid of those nasty outbreaks.

- **Take care of your lips.** No woman is going to want to kiss a pair of lips that are all chapped and cracked. Use lip balm regularly and stay hydrated.

- **Smoking.** If you smoke, it's a personal choice, but do realize that it is a health hazard and also makes your breath smell and your fingers or teeth yellow. Fewer people smoke every day, and the odds are against you if you continue. Consider giving it up.

- **Keep the sunglasses off.** Women want to see your eyes and to look into them when you are speaking. They don't want to see their own reflections.

Your Body Language

Stand in front of a mirror. Take a deep breath and stand relaxed.

How do you look?

Do you slouch? Are you standing tall? Shoulders back? Do you automatically cross your arms in front of your chest?

Your body language and how you present your self can be very important.

It's going to be different for everyone. We all have our physical strengths as well as our weakness, both ones we can change and ones we cannot. Be aware of what physical traits you have to your advantage and what ones you might want to work on.

- Eye contact. Look into her eyes, but don't stare. It's a fine line.

- Always turn towards the person you are talking to.

- Don't fidget. If you are standing, place your weight evenly on both feet.

- Stand up straight and don't slouch. It can make you come across as defeated or less masculine. And pull those shoulders back.

- Don't back away if she moves toward you. It sends a message of lack of interest, confidence or worse can signal you are timid.

- Don't clench your jaw. Relax. It's also known that if you part your lips a little bit while listening, women see this as interest.

- Tilt your head while listening to her. It shows you are listening to what they are talking about.

- Smile. A real smile. It shouldn't be too hard. Don't force it, but let it come out when you hear something pleasant, funny or sweet.

How to Enter a Room

It's been said so many times before: you only get one chance to make a first impression. But did you know that first impression is usually made long before you even know who you are going to talk to?

Women can be very detail-oriented, and that includes who is coming and going from a bar, restaurant or just in and out of a crowded room. They know who just walked in and have already started formulating an opinion the moment they saw them.

So, you need to remember that you need to be "On" from the moment you enter a room. It's not any different than a sporting event. The moment you leave that locker room, it's on, and you need to have your game face going.

Be ready before you enter any room. Shake off any negative thoughts and make sure you don't look angry or upset. Relax your face, rub out the muscles if you have to.

Also, give yourself a quick once over. Make sure your fly isn't open, your shirt is tucked in, and you don't accidentally have toilet paper on the bottom of your shoe.

Try this. Look at that door before you. Behind it is an opportunity. Every time you go somewhere, you have the opportunity to meet and flirt with women. That right there should put a smile on your face.

Don't slink into the room with your head down like you are trying not to be noticed. Walk in, head held high and shoulders back.

Keep your arms at your sides or out to greet people. As you enter, acknowledge people with a smile and a solid handshake. Be confident and warm.

Approaching Women

I'm 6'4". So, when I approach a woman, I have to be very aware that sometimes they are a bit scared by my size. Usually, it works to my advantage because the majority of women like a man they feel can protect them. The old "knight in shining armor" sort of fantasy. It's opened up a lot of conversations, and I didn't have to do a thing.

However, sometimes women get a bit scared initially. So, I have learned to add a nice smile, never tower over them or put them in a position where they may feel vulnerable. I want them to feel that they are talking to a protector.

If you are a big guy, try kneeling down next to them if they are sitting. By doing this, you don't seem threatening, and it puts them in an almost even eye level or even maybe a bit above you. This creates a psychological influence on her, making her more comfortable and she is more likely to let her guard down a bit. Don't just sit next to them uninvited, though.

Don't be frantic with your movements. Don't flail or rock back and forth on your feet. Just retain a calm body position.

Keep your hands out of your pockets. To a woman, this is a sign that you are uncomfortable or lack confidence. And don't place them on your hips or behind your back like a soldier at attention. She's going to think you are strange. Stand up straight. Shoulders back. Good posture.

Take normal steps. Don't rush or move strangely with little steps or even trying to approach being cute. You know what I mean, we've seen the guys who try a little dance as they cross the room to a girl. They're trying to be cute and charm her before they have even arrived.

Do you know what she's thinking right then? "What's the easiest excuse to get me out of talking to this goofball?" So, just approach her with confidence.

Shaking her hand is ok, but don't grasp it rough like you might with a man. Just take it gently but firmly, shake it a couple of times and release it. Don't stand there holding it while you talk. Also, some guys do the whole kissing the hand thing, and honestly, it doesn't work very often. It almost always comes off as insincere, juvenile or just creepy. Very few guys can pull it off, so I suggest just avoid it.

Clothing

The clothes that you wear will make a big difference in the way that others react to you. Some of the things that you should consider when picking out clothes to impress the woman includes:

Clean Clothes

If you are coming back from playing softball with your friends or you just helped build a house for the homeless, that's one thing. But if you are going out to a bar and wearing your lucky shirt even though it has a messy stain on it and hasn't been washed in weeks, it's time to rethink how you choose your clothes. Make sure your clothes are clean down to your underwear.

Well Fitted

Women love clothes that fit well and accentuate your body in the right way. Avoid sloppy, baggy jeans and shirts that are way too big or small. Remember, they like to see the goods that you've got, just like you do theirs.

Dress Like You Care

Dress in a way that shows you take pride in yourself. You don't have to wear a three-piece suit but show that you understand that you know how to present yourself maturely and professionally.

Dress Appropriately for the Event or Occasion

Part of being a real man is knowing how to fit into certain occasions. It's always great to show a bit of personal flair, but you don't show up to a wedding in shorts and flip-flops. Women want to know they will be proud to be seen with you and not embarrassed by what you do or dress.

Your Attitude and Behavior

Within a few moments, a woman is going to be able to tell a lot about you. She knows if you have a chance of having sex with her. Even in speaking a few simple sentences, your attitude will come out quickly.

When someone who is full of themselves and a bit of a jerk talks to a woman, she'll identify him and shut him down in mere moments. The same is with positives. If you show her attitudes she likes, she'll respond and open up to you.

- **Know what you want**. If you don't want something, be able to say "no" firmly but politely. Women love a man who knows what he wants but isn't a jerk about it.

- **Independence.** Women like it when you have outside activities, work, and other things. Independence shows them that you know who you are and where you are going in life.

- **The way you treat other people.** Women watch how you interact with other people. Are you nice to them to their face and then talk about them behind their back? Are you bitter about people? How do you treat waitresses and other service staff? How do you treat homeless people or the less advantaged? Women notice all of this and take mental notes.

- **The way you treat and talk about your mother.** It's true. Women draw a lot of conclusions about how you treat women and how you will treat her by how you talk about your mother. So, make sure you speak very highly of dear old mom.

- **Strong but sweet.** They don't want to see you cry but showing a little bit of softness or caring goes a long way. Even something as simple as smiling at a child or petting a dog can show her that you have a sweet side.

Chivalry

No, it is not dead. It's just shifted a bit.

The word chivalry came from the Middle Ages and was a code of honor that knights kept in relation to the way they lived their lives and how they treated the women of the kingdom.

In the Modern Era, it has become known as the way men treated women with respect by taking off their hats, standing when they got up or arrived at a table, opening doors and other acts of respect. In recent years, many of these acts have become labeled as sexist and demeaning to women, but new rules of chivalry have not been created. Men must create their own.

My grandmother was one of the biggest supporters of modern chivalry that you would have ever met. From a young age, she drilled it into me to open doors for women, walk on the street side of the sidewalk and other issues. If I failed to do what I should have as a chivalrous young man, I would often receive a firm tap on my shoulder from grandma.

I've learned to use this as a sort of flirting mechanism. When walking with women down the street, I will walk on the inner side and suddenly cross to the street side, explaining that my grandmother taught it to me and if she caught me right now, I'd get thwacked upside the head. Almost universally, I get a smile from the woman.

The reason this works for me is that in modern society, it's become a little dicey when to go over the top and do things for a woman that, until a few years ago, were the norm. Now we live in a sort of a gray area where men don't know if they should hold a door for a woman. I myself have even gotten snapped at for opening the door for a woman who announced she didn't need a man's help.

I look at it this way: be a human being. I would open the door for man as well just to be courteous. It's rude to let it hit them in their face, man or woman. If a woman snaps at you, just smile and go on with your day. And don't get indignant if a woman holds the door open for you instead. Politeness does not see gender or outdated gender roles.

The rule now is just don't be misogynistic. Don't treat women like they are weak, or it's something you are doing because they are a woman or because they are punier or need your assistance.

Do it because it's the civil way to live in society. Secretly, I believe most women still like it as long as you are being cool about it.

Your Brain

Have you ever heard that the brain is the largest sex organ in the body? It's true, and you need to make sure you put some effort into filling it before you head out into the dating world.

You don't have to be brilliant by any means. What I mean is be well read. Know what's going on in current events and the world. You don't need to spout out the latest headlines, but you need to be able to carry a conversation or have some knowledge that she didn't know.

Gather some facts and trivia. Don't become that annoying guy at trivia night who knows all the answers and mocks others because they don't. Being able to throw out some interesting facts from time to time can help you make a deeper mental connection with a woman.

Just don't become "that guy." Be careful of starting sentences with "Did you know..." It can come off as condescending and put the woman off. Try something like "You know, I heard once..."

Throw a few fun statistics in your brain. Make a few of them fun and sexy then look for the right opportunity to slip them into the conversation.

Most importantly, make sure that you have some information on a wide variety of subjects. You never know what a woman might find interesting. The more varied your facts and statistics, the greater your odds will be that you can think of something that will catch her fancy. Yet make sure you also have some degree of interest in your trivia. Otherwise, you'll start attracting women that you won't have anything in common with, and your flirtations will fizzle out as quickly as they were sparked.

Chapter 5: Finding the Right Women

So, you are ready to go flirt with some women, right? But where**?**

Where can you find the woman who is right for your interests? And when you find her, how you can tell that it's worth approaching her?

Where Do I Look?

Well, my first answer would be... everywhere**!**

Women are all around us, and so is the opportunity to talk with them and flirt. Sure, some places are going to have more openings than others, but you should always be open to opportunity. It could be waiting for a bus, at the gym or just walking down the street. If you see someone you're interested in; then there is an opportunity!

However, there are definitely some places where you might meet women and have a better opportunity to flirt with them. I saved some of the obvious (and sometimes tougher) ones for a special place in later chapters, but here are some where you can have some luck.

Karaoke

No, hold on, I'm serious. A lot of people think karaoke bars are cheesy, but that can be part of the fun. Everyone tends to make a bit of a fool out of themselves, and when you add a bit of alcohol, it creates a loose atmosphere where people are more likely to have fun and let their guard down.

I would definitely suggest that unless you are a professional singer, you don't serenade the bar with "American Pie" or some other long song. Keep it short and fun.

Hotel Bars and Lounges

Many people who are travelling are lonely or happy to meet new people. A lounge is a great place to meet women and talk and practice your new flirt skills.

Many times, women who are having a drink in a hotel bar are older and used to having conversations as part of their career. Your confidence level should be higher because you know your odds of striking up a conversation and flirting are better.

Flirting in a bar can be difficult. You are meeting someone new, the noise is loud (especially if there is music), and you want to make sure that you give off a good impression and not creep your interest out. But how do you make sure to get your point across when you have to shout every word? Do you offer to buy them a drink or let them get their own? What are the rules when flirting in any loud place? Some of the tips that you can follow when flirting in a bar includes:

1. Smile and make eye contact. This is a very simple method that you can use to show your interest, without saying anything.

2. Walk up to someone and start a conversation. Maybe ask them what their favorite team was as an ice breaker. Show your interest.

3. Sit next to the person and casually bump their arm. This is automatically going to get them to look up at you, which provides you with an opening to speak with them. You can then apologize for bumping into them and offer to buy them a drink. This lets the drink stay in their hand (you can never be too careful these days) while also opening the door to more conversation.

4. Use humor. Even if you are not able to speak up much or use different ones of voices in what you want to tell the other person, you can still use humor. Engage her by laughing at some of your own dance moves or tell them a good joke. The point here is to loosen the other person and get them to laugh with you. If they don't laugh, then you know they aren't interested, and you can walk away.

5. Ask them to dance. This is an easy way to figure out if they are interested in you. If they say no, then it is time to move on.

Flirting in a bar or a night club can be difficult, but being persistent and creative can make it easier for you to see the results that you want without feeling too awkward.

Meetups

For some people, it's much easier to have the structure of a pre-planned event. Someone else plans everything so you can just meet people and have fun.

This takes the pressure off and can help people relax and interact without having to concentrate on the actual event. Plus, you share common interests by being there, so it creates automatic things to open up conversations.

Cultural Events

Attending an event that has a cultural connection to you gives you the opportunity to meet women with the same background or at least an interest. Festivals, fairs, and parades are great places to have common ground to start chatting.

Art and Intellectual Events

Things like museums, art galleries, book readings, and signings are great events to meet women. Make sure you have some knowledge about what you are there for. Don't make the mistake of blowing an opportunity because you just spouted off information about the wrong artist.

What Are the Signs?

So, how do you know if she is open to talking and flirting?

First and foremost, look for body language symbols. We are going to continue to come back to body language, both hers and yours because it is one of the most important things in interacting with women.

Does she look closed off? Is she smiling? Does she look like she's ready to rip someone's head off?

Is she making eye contact with you? If she looks at you and looks away and doesn't look back, she's probably not for you.

But did you catch her checking you out? That's a major sign! If she was looking you up and down with a small smile, you just caught her checking you out. Try to lock eyes with her and send her a smile back. Once you do, head on over and say hello. It's a great opportunity to tease her or make a joke about catching her looking.

The Self Touch

It's been proven psychologically that when women are interested in a man, they tend to touch certain parts of their body. Some women with twist or play with their hair while others will touch their neck. It's up to you, however, to decide if you are causing the reaction or you just caught her scratching at an itch. Couple the touching with eye contact, and signs look good.

You Keep Running into Her

If a woman is interested, she may provide you opportunities. Do you think it's just chance that you keep running into her around the party or event? It might be, or it might be that she's been circling you trying to find the opportunity to flirt and chat. Take advantage of it! In fact, try some flirting and mention it. Try asking her if she's been following you.

The same with a bump or brushing past you. Yeah, sure, it might be accidental, but one lesson I can pass along to all of you from my experience... women are not stupid. They know exactly how to play the game and give you just enough information to give you the opportunity. This could also be a test, and she's seeing how much of a man you are. Will you talk to her?

She Talks to You

If she's interested, she might start the conversation. It might be something casual like asking about your coffee or some small talk, but she wouldn't have talked to you if she didn't want a response. Think about it. There are guys all around, and she talked to you. That's awesome!

Or she could be as forward as the woman I mentioned who was turned on by my name. Some women won't wait for you to come to them, but you better be ready.

So, don't freeze. Don't say anything stupid or creepy, just smile and answer her. Be casual and nice. Try to advance the topic in a fun, flirty way, but don't get into a major philosophical discussion. After some back-and-forth, make sure to introduce yourself if you haven't already.

What Are the Signs to Avoid?

Sarcasm

There is a difference between sarcasm and teasing, but sometimes it's hard to tell the difference. If you start talking to a woman and everything she says rolls off her tongue with a bit of venom and some of her comments sting a bit, it doesn't mean you are being soft skinned.

You might want to take a pass because if she flirts back, odds are it's going to be a rough ride without a pleasurable payoff.

The Money Honey

They used to call them gold diggers, but we all know the type. She doesn't care about anything but your car, your clothes, and your money. She'll expect you to pick up her bar bill as well as splurge for drinks for her friends.

She may laugh at every joke, bat her eyes at you and smile seductively, but chances are she's going to soak you for a lot of cash, and you won't even leave with her number. If she does go out with you, she's going to expect to be treated like a princess and may still not even give you a kiss.

Sometimes I'll call these women "plastic" due to the fake smile, plastic surgery, and the superficial outfit complete with designer label purses and clothing (and of course she makes sure everybody can see and notice them.) On top of that, I find their attitudes and general personality fake, adding to the moniker "plastic."

The Crazy One

I think we toss this phrase around too much, but I will admit I am guilty. The psycho, the crazy. Often, we use it as a label for a specific thing they did, but there are women out there who rightfully deserve the title.

Be careful of the women who latch on too quickly and who make strange comments but claim to just be joking. If they start to tell stories about how they burned down their ex-boyfriend's house but it was just a "misunderstanding," it might be time to cut your losses and walk away.

The Drunk

I used to work in a popular college bar, and every night some drunk girl would come up to me and flirt and I would flirt back. However, since I was working, I will admit flirting was part of my job. I would constantly be asked to go grab a drink at their place after work or go to an after-hours bar or party.

I will not make a move on a girl if she has been drinking and I haven't. I would always get numbers and meet them for coffee or dinner when both of us were sober. Let me tell you, that built up some serious trust when we did meet up.

Be careful of the drunken girl. You might think that you are making progress but realize that she's not hearing you properly and most likely one of her friends is going to come to get her and pull her away. But most of all, odds are she's going to go home, pass out and barely remember that you ever even talked to her.

The Hot Attention Seeker

You see them at every bar. The highly attractive woman with the large breasts put out on display, the perfect make-up and the near-perfect fluttering of eyelashes. These are women who feed on attention and flirting.

A lot of times, these women already have boyfriends but go out to soak up all the admiration and flirting they can before they go back to their man. They want to be the center of attention but try to pretend that they really don't want to be. They'll flirt back a bit, but they are like parasites that want your attention but aren't going to give you anything back. Avoid them as soon as you see the signs.

Fishing for Compliments

Similar to the hot attention seeker, women who are fishing for compliments just want someone to tell them that they're pretty, smart, funny, worth-while, etc. These women will say things like "God, I hate this dress, I look so fat in it", "I wish I weren't so stupid", or "Why can't I look like *her*? She's so beautiful and I'm so plain". They might also take selfies and caption them with things like "I'm so ugly" or "I'm so fat". Most of the time, they're doing this for the purpose of getting people to contradict them.

If you start flirting with a woman like this, you could be in for quite the trip. Like the hot attention seeker will use people for attention, women who fish for compliments will use you for the compliments that will inevitably come with your flirting. Rather than get any flirting and compliments back—except for the occasional, and sometimes insincere, "you're too sweet"—you'll only get her pushing back on your compliments so that you'll give her more.

Women who fish for compliments aren't necessarily bad people, but they can become desperate and are often dealing with a lot of emotional issues. They could even be carrying psychological trauma that has given them low self esteem and made them reliant on the praise of others for their own confidence. Sadly, these kinds of issues can plague anyone, so you won't be able to know if

you're flirting with someone fishing for compliments until you're being sucked in. Once you realize what's happening, don't be rude. Just think of
a polite reason to leave, wish her the best, and
part ways.

Chapter 6: The Mechanics of Flirting

So, that's all well and good, but what you want to know is how it works, right?

There are many parts to flirting and the way each individual aspect works. So, let's break it down into individual pieces.

How to Flirt with Words

Use Descriptive Words

In the old days, you would have needed to write a poem or sonnet in order to woo a girl properly. I know I'm glad those days are over. I may have many skills, but poetry is not one of them.

This doesn't mean you can't use the right words to impress her while you flirt. Use words that have deeper meanings. Not necessarily innuendo, that's a different subject, but words that are more descriptive and that will resonate in her mind and heart.

- **"Want"**- instead of simply saying you want something (or her) try descriptive words like **"yearn," "crave" or "desire."**

- **"Turned On"**- try something like **"aroused"** or maybe even more descriptive like **"on fire."** Don't say **"That's hot."** Paris Hilton has ruined that phrase for all time.

- **"Dirty"**- try a word like "**risqué**." Not only does it sound fancier, but it's also actually a sort of historic fun word to use. It creates a picture of lush and old-fashioned bordellos and naughty times. That's a good thing. **"Frisky"** is another fun word that has playful overtones. Watch for her reaction to test if you can go further with sexual conversation.

- **"Sexy"**- Before saying something is sexy, see if the word **"sensual"** will work. It's much deeper and more mature.

- **"Like/interest"**- try saying something like "I have a real **passion** for..." Whether it's your work, your hobbies or women, by using the word passion, it shows both respect and the desire behind it.

Teasing

Teasing is great because it actually brings you closer. It's similar to how you might tease your best friends or a sibling or family member, that teasing actually shows that you have enough of a connection to give them some good-natured ribbing.

With flirting, it's the same thing. It will bring you closer, break down barriers and provide an opportunity to talk about other fun subjects including sex.

How to Tease

Use your voice and hands. If you make it a bit over-the-top and laugh and smile when you do it, she'll know you are just being playful, not cruel.

Always be very observant as to how she reacts. Some women love a good tease and will give it right back, while others don't like it as much. They'll smile at one or two good jabs but might not be interested in too much more. Part of good flirting is always knowing how to adjust your approach.

Get more personal as the conversation progresses. Part of the fun of flirting is seeing how it becomes more intimate as you are being successful. Don't start off teasing her about sex, but if you can tell it's going well between you, then it's time to begin to make jokes.

Look for opportunities to tease nicely based on what she says. If she says she's very clumsy, then use that. It's information that she gave you, and she jokes about it herself. So, it shows her that not only do you share her sense of humor you've been listening to her.

Don't tease her about things that she might be sensitive about. Stay away from certain topics like her weight or a pimple or blemish. Also, don't start ripping into her choices of past boyfriends. This will just make you sound petty and mean. Even if she makes jokes about an ex, be careful before you tease her about him.

Don't tease her constantly. Use it sparingly. Have a conversation that also includes serious talk and listening as well as some jokes with the teasing. Nobody wants to be made fun of all the time, no matter how playful it might be.

Accuse Her of Being the Aggressive One

Make jokes about her hitting on you or having dirty thoughts and saying something inappropriate. It gives you a chance to switch roles on her since men are usually being accused. It's also a great way to break the ice for more sexually suggestive topics and test her reaction.

Mimic Her Playfully

Find something in the way that she speaks or physical trait that you can mimic. If she got upset at something you said, maybe make a pouty face back at her. If she has a sense of humor, she'll laugh. Her reaction will tell you a lot.

Be careful with this one. There are some types of speech and even physical traits that are going to be there because of a physical issue. The woman could be sensitive about it. This means that she won't want someone pointing it out. For example, do not mimic them if they are lisping.

Give Her A Nickname

Something cute or funny but not insulting or creepy. Something that has to do with one of her qualities that you like. Her laugh or her smile. And especially avoid things like "sweetheart", "sweet cheeks", or any other number of patronizing nicknames you hear womanizers spew off at random. They're not cute, they're demeaning.

How to Build Chemistry

Natural Chemistry

Sometimes you just get lucky. You walk into a room and lock eyes with a woman, the pheromones are raging, and it's obvious that you are both interested.

Within a few words, you both know that there is electricity between the two of you. It falls into a natural flirtatious conversation, and after a few minutes, you both know this is going somewhere.

But I hate to tell you, it isn't always like this. Most of the time, you are going to need to put in a bit of work to either get the sparks flying or to stoke the fire.

"The Spark"

Men and women are wired differently. It's not a moral judgment; it's just a fact.

As men, we are very physical and visually stimulated. What we see gets us turned on. Yes, there are romantic and mental elements, but biologically we have been wired for millions of years to see what we want and go after it.

Women have a different trigger. They need to feel **"The Spark."**

A lot of things can set this off. It can be purely sexual, a combination of physical and mental attraction. Or the spark can be caused by some of the other things we have discussed. Protection, security and procreation and the primal needs the female brain searches out.

But they need that spark, and if it isn't generated automatically, you need to push it along.

In order to nurture this spark, you need to talk and flirt with her in a way that doesn't feel superficial. She needs to believe that the things you are saying you have never said to another woman before. She wants you in the moment with her.

For example, after a few minutes, she tells you that she is a teacher. How do you follow up on this?

You could comment on her liking to work with children or having summers off or even about how she is admirable for taking a low paying job that is so fulfilling. And she'll smile and lose interest in you.

Do you see the problem with these questions?

You are asking her superficial (and common) questions she's heard many times before. They're not really about her; they are about her job. This will not foster a spark. You need to get past that and find her connection.

So instead, consider asking her about <u>why</u> she became a teacher, what she likes best about it. Get to her feelings, and you will be stoking that spark.

How to Give a Real Compliment

You need to understand that women are used to compliments. They have been getting them since boys were old enough to notice them and they have become very adept at learning what real compliments are and what are basically just pickup lines.

Make sure that you understand the difference between a compliment and a comment. A comment is just that… a comment. When you say, "Those are beautiful eyes/legs, lips, etc.," you aren't actually complimenting the woman for something, you are just commenting on her.

It's really not any different than a golf commentator watching a pro golfer sink a put and saying "And he knocks it into the hole for par." **You are stating the obvious, just like every other guy. You need to set yourself apart.**

Compliment her on things that are different or unique to her. Instead of just saying "You have beautiful eyes," compliment the flecks or the way they change color. This tells her that it's not just a general sexual based comment, but you are actually noticing something about her that is unique.

And don't just compliment something that she has no control over. If you tell her she has a great body, first of all, it's going to sound pretty creepy. Second, unless she spends hours at the gym and is creating a professional fitness body, she's probably not going to take it as well. She might have issues of her own or just think it's a sexual comment.

Compliment her on the choices she makes and things that add to her personality and style. Compliment her on her dress choice, her jewelry or the way she styled her hair (not just the hair in general.)

Specifics that are something she did or put time into will always be taken better and as genuine. She put effort into something, and you noticed. That's a win.

How to Create and Use a Hook

When I was in college, I had two friends in college named Jack and Louie. They would often go out to the bars because they thought this was the best way to meet girls. Jack would talk to them because he was pretty good at flirting.

Louie would sit a bit away from them but still within talking range. Jack would motion to Louis, saying he was a little shy about a physical abnormality he had. The girls would look and try to figure out what it was and finally Jack would tell them.

"Don't look, but he's got a cock below his knee," Jack would say. The girls would always gasp or not believe, and finally, Jack would motion over to Louis who would lift up his pant leg to reveal a big rooster tattoo he had on his calf.

The girls would laugh, groan and shake their heads, but they always ended up hanging out with them.

This was their hook. I will admit, it is a bit creative and could even be considered over-the-top, but it worked for them.

If you come up with something that's good, of course, use it. If you have something unusual that you do or have achieved, find a way to work it into the conversation or use it to break the ice.

Another one many people have used to great success is becoming an ordained minister. You can do it online for a few dollars, and it's always a fun way to open up a conversation.

Just stay away from the ones that have been run into the ground. Please for the sake of all men out there, no more:

- Card or magic tricks

- Snakes, iguanas or other animals on your shoulder

- Pretending you work in show business and can make her famous

- Lying about any line of work to impress her (police officer, soldier, firefighter, etc.)

- Bad t-shirts with puns

- Outlandish outfits that are only meant to draw attention

How to Subtly Exaggerate

Embellishing a little bit is normal. It might be on your resume, or what you told your friends about a fish you caught or when you are talking to a woman. But there is a difference between lying and exaggerating.

If you are telling a woman that you drive a Ferrari, live in a penthouse condo and spend your vacations in the South of France when you actually have an old Honda, can barely make your rent and are lucky to make it to the lake for a vacation, then you are lying. Women hate lies.

If you are exaggerating a bit, that's different. If you exaggerate, it needs to be something that is not going to come back at you if you get caught. You want to exaggerate in a way that it's their perception that shapes what they believe just based on the way you told them. Often, it's not as much exaggerating as being vague.

If you are talking to a woman and she asks what you do, you could say that you work in the entertainment industry. She may assume you are an actor, a writer, director or anything else when, in reality, you work on the catering truck and make sandwiches for the crew. Eventually what you really do might come out, but any preconceptions she had were hers.

If you are telling a story, you might want to jazz it up a bit by adding some small exaggerations. Did you get caught on a boat in a storm once? Well, as you are retelling the story, make that storm a bit bigger. Don't let this go too far. If you exaggerate too much, you will end up with a woman who knows you are lying and will wonder how much you lie in other things. But telling a bit of an exaggeration, especially if you can get them to laugh and enjoy it more, can be a good thing.

How to Use Sexual Innuendo

I love this category. I'm a big fan of wordplay and turning a phrase. And it's not that difficult, but men seem to screw it up all the time.

Innuendo is just about ambiguous language. That means that certain words and phrase can be turned into a different sexual, fun and playful meaning.

However, the best use of this is when you can do it subtly. The subtler or more based on a misunderstanding, the funnier it can be and the more likely she is going to enjoy it. Also, please remember, if you just come out with dirty jokes, this is not innuendo.

The Misunderstanding

I use this one a lot to great success. A woman will make an innocent statement, but there will be one word that can be taken in a number of ways. I will pretend to take it sexually and then tease her about going too fast, or she's just interested in one thing. The woman will laugh and tell me that's not true.

This is a great place for a little test of how things are going. At this point if she reaches over and playfully slaps you on the arm, you know she's enjoying the conversation and is playing along.

The goal is to get her to join in as well. If you show that you are a healthy, sexual male who can offer up some clever innuendo but realize that the more there is to flirting in conversation, the more likely she is to join in the fun.

Touching

Touching while you are flirting is so incredibly important, but it can be very dangerous, especially in today's society.

I was at a bar recently having a drink with a few friends when I noticed a guy start chatting with a woman at another table. He was pleasant-looking, well-dressed but not too cocky. As he started to talk to the woman, he smiled and so did she. He looked like he was doing well. I even offered him a mental attaboy as I watched.

Then it happened. After less than a couple minutes of chatting, he reached over and held her hand. He was still smiling and still friendly, but her face changed immediately. She became stone-faced, pulled her hand back and stared at him. Suddenly, her body language changed, her arms and legs crossed. She completely closed off to him. After another minute, he knew it wasn't working and he left her to her drink.

He made a major mistake. He moved in way too soon.

It can be difficult to judge when is the right time to make physical contact. Sometimes you think you have a signal she'll be ok with it, but you read it wrong. But then some women don't mind if you touch them from the moment you say hello.

I believe you should always err on the side of caution, but that doesn't mean you need to be timid.

Pat her hand or arm, but don't do it strangely or like a creep. Use it as punctuation to what you are saying. Maybe you are telling a story, and you can tap her hand, saying, "And do you know what he did?" This brings her into the story while you are making a connection. Make sure to watch for her reaction. If she pulls away when you tap her arm, make a note of it.

If she seems comfortable with touch, incorporate it with other forms of flirting like teasing. Give her a gentle push or a little nudge on the arm when you make a joke or tease her. Be sure to give her a wink when you do it, though, to let her know that you're just teasing. Also be sure not to use this to often, or else she'll think that you only think of her as "one of the guys" and don't have any sexual interest in her.

Hair

I love this one, and it has worked for me many, many times. I'll notice that they have a hair out of place or something in their hair. It doesn't have to be real. I'll mention it and ask if it's ok if I fix it. Don't just start touching a woman and getting into their personal space without asking first, no matter how well you know them. Almost every time they say yes, and I'll gently smooth out their hair or pretend to flick away a piece of lint or something.

I'm telling you, this one is a great one. A couple of times I actually heard the women moan when I did it. I kid you not.

Encourage Her to Touch You

I used to live in Chicago and would meet a lot of women from Michigan. In Michigan, because of the shape of the state, they use their hand to show where they live. I would always hold up my hand and ask them to show me where they lived in the state. They would touch my palm and often trace lines to the different places they had lived, creating more contact between us.

There's also activity. If she mentions that you are probably big enough to pick her up, offer to do it. If she makes a comment about not wanting to walk, playfully offer for her to jump on your back for a piggyback ride. If you're getting out of a car or getting off the final step on a set of stairs, offer your hand to help her down.

Don't ask her to feel your muscles. If she asks, let her, but be somewhat embarrassed by it.

Cozying Up

This is a great one for a bar or somewhere where it might be cold, loud or great people-watching.

Turn the discussion toward people watching and move beside her so you can both watch the room. As you laugh and comment about what you see, get close so you can joke with each other. It creates an intimate atmosphere, and because your attention is focused outward, it's not going to create any discomfort. By being in this close proximity, it's going to make her feel more comfortable and lead to further touching.

Pay attention to their cues with this one. Closeness can really help to form that connection that you want, but some girls may be turned off from this. If you start to cozy up a bit, you may notice that they tense up and maybe shift away a bit.

When this happens, it is best to give them space. They might not be comfortable enough doing this yet with you and will want their space. Or maybe there is something in their past that makes them a bit uncomfortable.

Always take the woman's cue with this one. If they seem comfortable with you coming closer, then this is a great way to build that connection and get yourself stuck in their mind. Just don't push it past the limits that they are setting.

How to Flirt Without Saying a Word

While talking to a woman is probably the most effective way to flirt and get to know her, it is by no means the only way.

You can flirt without even saying a word! It has to do with simple non-verbal cues and body language.

- How you sit. Own your space. This can be seen as a sign of strength by women, and they will definitely notice. Don't lounge around like a slob but be comfortable where you sit. Don't hunch over. Be casual, but not rude. Don't put your feet up on the table. And absolutely no manspreading. If a woman has invented a chair just to make sure we can't do it, it's probably not something they want to see.

- Don't flash that million-dollar smile quite yet. Bring it down. When you catch each other's eyes, give her a small smile. She'll feel like it's just for her and your little secret, especially if you are talking to a group of people and took a moment to let her into your world.

- Make sure not to close yourself off. Don't huddle over or cross your arms over your body. Show her you are open to her by opening up your body language.

- Show off your manly side. By subtly touching certain parts of your body, it brings attention to them. Touch your jaw or scratch some scruff. Rub your biceps, but make sure it's an organic-looking move. You're not showing off, just quietly highlighting certain parts of your body.

- Be gentle. Women want men to be strong but not aggressive, so don't slam anything and always be gentle when you touch her. This is especially important when you're tall like me or just bigger overall. Women will feel more comfortable around a gentle giant who can protect her but knows how to reign it in than a he-man who treats everything like a test of his strength.

Don't Forget Her Friends

If you are talking to a specific woman and she is with a group of friends, don't alienate the rest of them and only speak to her. Be inclusive. Make sure to include everyone in the group, even though you are giving her the most attention.

Remember that at any point one of her friends might decide to step up and pull her away. They might decide that you aren't right for their friend, or it could even be a source of jealousy. It's all part of the friendship/sisterhood that women share.

So, make sure everybody in the group likes you, but don't be a sycophant or plastic. Don't just agree with everything and act like a puppy dog. Have genuine conversations with opinions and information, but don't dominate the conversation and don't lead it back to subjects that obviously were over.

Look for cues from her friends that it's working. They may mention her likes and dislikes or how she's looking for something in a man. Listen and make sure to act on these cues. If her friends like you, they will help. But if they decide they don't like you, they will protect their friend and shut you down.

How to Make Her Want to See You Again

You had a great conversation, and it really seemed like you hit it off. You want to ask for her number, but how can you make sure that she will be interested in giving it to you?

Be Honest and Trustworthy

You don't need to tell her your life story or everything you are doing, but don't lie to her face. If you say you are going to do something, do it. Even if it's little.

Find a way to let her know you are a man of your word. If you say you are going to text her, do it. If you say you'll send her an article you talked about, make sure you follow through.

Be Interesting

If you are boring, have nothing to discuss and aren't fun to be around, she's not going to want to want to see you again. It's a fact. Nobody wants to be around boring people. If you aren't interesting, she may be nice to you and talk, but she's not going to want to give you too much more of her precious time.

How do you know if you're being boring? Watch her as you talk. If her eyes are drooping, she's subtly checking her phone or watch or she's looking lazily around the room, then it's probably time for you to change your topic and possibly your whole approach.

Be a Little Mysterious

This is a part of being interesting. Don't give away everything about you up front. At least, make her think that there's something more to you that she'll want to know about. You might typically be a "what you see is what you get" kind of guy, and women appreciate that honesty, but they also like men who have some layers, and teasing at these layers gives her hope that she will never be bored in a relationship with you.

I travel a lot for work, and women love to hear stories about the different countries I've been to. One of my favorite things to do during one of my travel stories is to off-handedly mention a similar—or strikingly different—experience I had on another trip and say, "But that's a different story entirely." I'll then continue with my original story without returning to my other comment. Most often, the woman I'm talking to will ask me about the other story, to which I'll respond with something like "Maybe I'll tell you another time" or " I don't want to get into that right now, but give me your number and maybe I can call and tell you about it." This way, not only is she left with a little mystery that makes her want to learn more about me, but we'll also have an excuse to exchange numbers or e-mail addresses.

Be Comfortable

While you are hanging out, make sure you are comfortable to be around. Don't talk about topics she's not interested in or, worse, offended by. Make things easy. Don't talk about the stresses of a date (if that's what it is). Make it feel like talking to her is the easiest thing you've ever done.

Now, I'm not saying you need to be the life of the party, tell constant jokes or sing and dance. You just have to be you. Have good conversation, make her laugh and, most of all, make sure she's comfortable.

Do Something Scary

Have you ever gone to a scary movie with a girl and she jumps and grabs your hand?

If you do something scary like a horror film or a roller coaster, the endorphins are going to be released which is going to make you both excited. Because you did it together, the brain is going to connect the endorphins in her mind with you. And she's going to want more of that rush that she connects with you.

Do not take the word "scary" to extremes. Horror films, roller coasters, and even haunted house attractions work here because while the endorphins are released, the chances of you actually getting hurt aren't as great. Movies won't hurt us, roller coasters are regulated and operated by trained employees, and we trust that the actors at most haunted house attractions won't actually touch us. So, the "scary" associated with endorphin-releasing entertainment like these is not the same "scary" as when you, say, get into bar fight or walk down an unlit alley.

While you want to share a rush, you don't want her to connect that rush with something truly life-threatening or with you doing anything stupid.

No Pressure

Don't overwhelm her with what you are looking for in a woman or a relationship. Never tell her that she's exactly what you have been looking for or you could see the two of you spending a long life together.

This is not the talk that is going to make her want to see you again. Some women respond to this, but I'll be honest with you, they are looking to get married and have kids as soon as possible, which is fine, if that's what you are looking for, but that desperation can be misinterpreted.

Keep it casual. Just have fun. Don't try to put labels on things, even jokingly. Don't be distant, but keep a little intrigue going.

Push-Pull Flirting

Now, I am going to be honest with you, I don't use this method. It's just not the style that I like to flirt. That doesn't mean it won't be successful for you.

The idea behind push-pull is when you say something nice or compliment a woman and then follow it up with something that is less nice or possibly less flattering.

Then you follow it up with something that pulls you away verbally or physically. You can say something that limits what you said. It's basically playing games with her to keep her off balance. The idea is to create emotional connections and then distance. When you go on to the next connection, the distance you created allows her to move closer. It's sort of like fishing when you let out some line, reel the fish in and let them run a bit.

For example, you might say something like she has the most beautiful smile in the room but then follow up with a statement that says you were wrong there are a few beautiful smiles in the room and you would put hers in about third place. By doing this, you pulled her in and then pushed her away.

There are certain types of women who respond to this technique. They tend to crave attention and will take it in any form that they can get, so realize this.

For the most part, women do not like this technique. They can become highly offended and catty in a defensive way. So, it can backfire.

In fact, part of the reason I don't like this particular technique is because of what a former neighbor/current female friend told me about her experience with it.

One time, while at a club, she was chatting with this guy over at the bar, and he seemed like a decent enough fellow. Smart, witty, good-looking. After a couple drinks, she was kind of into him.

Then he drops a line saying, "You know, you have the most gorgeous eyes," pauses to take a drink, and continues, "even if the little one's a bit small."

This left my friend stunned, embarrassed, and furious all at once. She didn't see it as a compliment or a reason to continue talking with him. Instead, she stormed back to her friends and avoided him the rest of the night.

My friend also told me that for many women, it's akin to something called a "backhanded compliment". Essentially, a backhanded compliment is when someone says something like "you have such a pretty face, it's a shame that you hide it behind all that fat". Among women, this is done when they want to insult someone but do not want to or cannot let others see how much they dislike the other woman. While not exactly the same as push-pull flirting, many women associate the two, making it so that a lot of women do not respond well to push-pull flirting.

Many men and dating advisors highly recommend push-pull, but again, I don't. I think it is an unhealthy way to communicate and more often than not isn't going to get you the results or the type of woman you desire. I suggest you stick to the playful teasing and leave the mind games out of it.

However, a word of caution if you do choose to engage in this technique: you must be careful with the pullback you use. If you say or do something that's too harsh, you may trigger a defensive response. Needless to say, this would kill your entire game.

Chapter 7: The Dos and Don'ts of Flirting

So, we got through the mechanics and basics of flirting, but there are a lot of little things that you can do in order to be more effective. Also, there are several things that you plain avoid.

Follow these tips, and you will find your flirting and conversation efforts far more successful.

The Dos

- Know the difference between gentle teasing and an insult. Insulting her is not going to help you. Always be careful with the tone of language that you use.

- Do be proud of your accomplishments and life, but don't show off and brag.

- Know when it's not right and bow out gracefully. You can say you have to go, a friend is signaling for you or just smile and say nice meeting you and leave. But learn when to cut your losses and walk away.

- Be funny, but don't be a clown. Don't be overly physically comic or belittle yourself.

- Relax and not take yourself too seriously. First and foremost, flirting should be fun. You won't get a woman to talk to you look and act like you're off to war.

- Be friendly and nice to any friends she may be with, but make sure you aren't flirting with them as well. Find your target and stay focused. Although, if you find she isn't receptive and someone else is, there is nothing wrong with changing your target.

- If it's going well but you're there with friends, introduce them to her and either invite them into the conversation or tell them you'll be a while. Make sure that she can tell that she's still your focus even if they're around, but show her that you aren't some jerk who will just blow off his friends for a pretty face. She'll respect you for your loyalty.

The Don'ts

- Never say "Hey baby, sweetie, honey..." or any other "cute name." It's not cute. Don't do it.

- Don't crowd a woman. Be aware of personal space.

- Don't pull a move where you go around her back to get her number from a friend. Do it yourself. This isn't middle school.

- Never tell her to smile or that she would look prettier if she did.

- Never compare her to an angel, a building, or basically any other structure that leads to a line.

- You can flirt with a married woman, but part of being a true man is respecting another man's woman. A bit of friendly flirting is ok, but be very careful. The same goes with a woman who has a serious boyfriend or long-time partner.

- You can flirt with strippers, but realize that they are strippers. Their job is to make you feel good and cared for in exchange for money. Don't fall for their stage act.

- If you flirt with cashiers, baristas, and other customer service employees, don't take up too much of their time. You want to get them to like you and/or give them a good time, not get them in trouble with their managers or piss off the customers in line behind you.

- Don't send dick pics. Even when you are in a relationship, be careful. Not only do they offend too early on, remember she probably won't delete it, and it might start getting circulated.

- I shouldn't have to say this, but don't make any lewd gestures. You might think you're being funny, but you're not. It will really creep women out, and it will probably also get you a lot of nasty looks from the men around you, too. But that's only if you don't get thrown out of the building.

- Don't over compliment her. It will come off as disingenuous, and she is not going to believe you anymore.

- While you shouldn't forget your friends, don't let them influence you too much, either. Men tend to try and show off in front of their friends, especially when it comes to "catching" women. Don't. It makes us all look like pigs.

- Don't do anything with any strings attached. While you should be confident enough to believe that you will achieve your goal in flirting (whatever that might be), don't think that she has to do anything just because you bought her a drink and made her laugh. You're not entitled to anything.

A word of caution: While most places are generally suitable for flirting, there are specific circumstances under which you may wait for the woman to signal some kind of interest.

For instance, libraries, doctor's offices and even funeral homes seem like obvious places you might want to hold back somewhat. Also, keep in mind that not every occasion is suitable for flirting. While weddings seem like clichés, other occasions such as a court hearing might end up costing you some unwanted embarrassment.

A good rule of thumb to follow here is common sense. If the situation dictates itself, then by all means. Otherwise, being friendly and courteous might be your best bet.

In the next section, we are going to look at different situations of flirting that you may encounter. And if you like what you've learned so far, or you've found benefit, feel free to leave a review on Amazon. I really appreciate it as your feedback means a lot to me.

Part Three: Specific Situations

Chapter 8: Flirting Online

Flirting online isn't just a great way to move a woman's interest in you forward; it can be a lot of fun!

But before we get started, let's go over a few ground rules:

What Happens Online, Stays Online...Forever

In many ways, flirting online harkens back to when we were kids passing notes in class. You get the thrill of waiting for the response and that rush when it comes back and is positive and pushing the flirtation forward. However, just like these notes, virtual flirtations can come back to bite you in the butt. Now, though, your teacher catching you in the act and reading your note aloud is the least of your concerns.

When I was a kid and starting to date, my mother gave me great advice. She told me never to write something down, even in a note, or take a photo that you don't want the world to see. So, always be careful online, you never know who is going to see what you write. After all, even if something is deleted, it is stored somewhere, virtually forever.

Emoticons and Emojis

One quick note before we get started. Always be very careful about using emoticons and emojis. Feel free to use them, but don't overuse them. You don't need to finish your message with seven different types of smiley faces.

Also, be careful about using emojis with secret meanings. Not only could you offend, but quite honestly, they may not know what you are saying. To some people, an emoji of an eggplant is just an emoji of an eggplant.

On the other hand, always make sure you know all the meanings yourself. I have known several older texting flirters that didn't realize there were other meanings behind certain emoticons and get themselves into some embarrassing situations.

Proceed with Caution

You have to be just as careful approaching women online as you are in real life, maybe even more, for both their sake and yours. You never know whom you're speaking with online, nor do they. You might think that you're talking with some beautiful twenty-year-old college student on Twitter only to find out that it's some forty-five-year-old scumbag with nothing better to do with his time than troll people online. You must also beware of scams, bots, and predators.

And remember, every online danger you have to look out for is one that she'll be cautious of, too. In fact, for women, it can be even more dangerous, so they'll be even more careful whom they talk to. Just keep this in mind and be patient; so long as you're being genuine with her and she's truly interested, she'll open up.

Of course, there's more than just safety that you need to consider when striking up a virtual conversation with a woman. I'll get into the best ways for each kind of online interaction below, but there's one rule that's universal to all platforms: NO PICKUP LINES.

We already discussed this earlier this book, but there's an extra level of creepiness—and, sometimes, embarrassment—that comes with online pickup lines. In chat, e-mail, and text messages, a woman can't see your body language. She won't have any way to know for sure if you're teasing, flirting, serious, or an idiot. She only has the words on her screen to go by. Your intentions are at the mercy of her interpretation. More often than not, a pickup line that you think is cute or clever will come off as stupid or creepy—many times both.

Texting

Make sure you are moving the conversation forward. Don't dwell on topics for too long or it may sound like you are obsessing, and she'll be done with you. If a joke falls flat, move on.

The idea is to engage the woman by asking questions or making statements that she'll want to respond to and keep the conversation going. Always keep your texts simple and direct. You want her to understand exactly what you mean and not think you meant something else. Much is lost in texting, even with the use of emojis. Don't read too much in between the lines.

If you use innuendo, keep it fun and light and touch on the sexual humor but don't dive into it. Be careful about sending suggestive photos and memes. Make sure she has a similar sense of humor.

Try making plans in a text with a definitive activity. For example, don't just say "Want to grab a movie sometime?" It's passive, and women don't respond to passive. They like it when there is a definitive question they can answer yes or no to.

So instead you could text "I am really interested in that new comedy that came out this week. Want to go see it Friday night?"

Waiting to Call or Text

Ahhhh... the eternal question.... Should I wait a certain number of days to text or call?

My feeling is this: as long as you don't overwhelm her, you can text any time, but the more you do, the less you are giving her time to think about you. It's sorta counterintuitive, isn't it? You would think that the more you text her, the more she would think of you, right?

You have to let her miss you. You have to let her brain begin to create a fantasy around you by filling in the blanks.

Here's the male example: Have you ever seen a woman walking toward you on the street? You can't quite make out all her features, so your brain fills in the details to make her as beautiful as possible. Then she moves closer, and you can see more, and it wasn't what you imagined. Closer and closer. She may be beautiful, but she's not what you imagined in your head.

Texting a woman is a bit of the same. Let her create the image of you in her head from the message and photos. If you text her too much, you could be creating a problem. Now she has more information, but it's not face-to-face. She's going to start creating a picture, and it might not go in your favor.

However, this can cause a dilemma. You don't want that fantasy she is creating to grow too big and take on a life of its own. You don't want to sit down for a date, and suddenly she realizes you are nothing like what she created in her mind. So, don't wait too long to move from texting to spending time together in person.

If you've already met and created a dialogue, now you have a foundation that you can riff on, joke and tease. You can push things further, using innuendo with the information you gathered from meeting in person.

It's ok to make jokes about sex, but don't make it the crux of your conversation. Use it as a tester, but don't dwell on it.

Don't send multiple texts before you get a response, and never ask "are you there?" or other comments that sound can be taken as creepy. Also, double-check your spelling before you hit send.

Social Media

Social media has become an entirely new area for flirtation, and there are a whole new set of rules on how to do it properly.

Each platform has its own best way to interact and flirt, but here's one rule across the board.

Keep it happy. Keep your personal issues, bad days, gripes and political views off social media if you want people to respond to you. Women don't want to see your bad days. They want to see a virile male who has the world by the tail. Yeah, we all have bad days and failures, but social media isn't the place to air your grievances.

Look at some of the most successful accounts out there. Sure, they're celebrities, and people follow them because they are famous, but you can learn from them. What do they have in common? Positive posts, uplifting and motivational. You don't have to sound like a life coach or self-help guru but keep it positive.

Presentation

We talked about how presenting yourself in person is important, but the same thing is true online.

On social media, make sure you use a good profile pic that shows you in a good light. It can be fun, but not one that makes you look stupid. In your profile description, put in pertinent information about yourself. Sound like a real person.

Instagram

Instagram is a great place to meet people and flirt online since it's a photo and text-based platform.

- Be careful with liking photos. Don't go through a woman's account and like a ton of them. It'll look desperate and a bit weird.

- Keep your photos current and fun. You want people to know that you have a cool life and that you are a real person. Too many old pics or staged ones might make people think you aren't real or trying to cover up for something.

- Be careful about digging into someone's past photos too much. By staying with recent pictures at first, they won't think you are burrowing into their past or getting a bit too involved. You might have an opportunity when they mention they took a certain type of photo in their timeline and then you can comment "I have to go see that!" and go back into their history.

- Leave clever comments but make sure it doesn't sound creepy or have some sort of hidden meaning that they won't get.

- Use Instagram stories. This is a neat feature because it disappears after 24 hours. You can post things that show your interests without seeming boastful or full of yourself. If there are things you share with your flirt friend, it's a chance to make connections without broadcasting to the world forever in your timelines.

- Wait for the response. Don't keep posting or messaging someone when you haven't heard back. Women will see this as desperation or possibly worse. Be patient.

- Make sure you are saying something interesting. Don't just make the same comments, jokes or statements. Make sure it's something that relates to them. Ask questions, use the back-and-forth to get to know them and find more information for more flirting and communication.

- Don't take it too seriously. Like all online flirtation, there is a sense of anonymity behind the keyboard. People are often more likely to type things they wouldn't say in person. To make sure not to be too serious. If you like the person and want to pursue it, move it to Facebook, direct messaging or even better... real life.

Twitter

While Twitter has become more of a political shouting ground over the last few years, it's still a great place to communicate and flirt. Because you are limited to only a certain number of characters, it forces you to get creative with limited words.

You always want to be careful not to step over the line, or on a lot of places you can get banned or they can spread something to the Twitterverse. Don't DM her a photo you wouldn't want the world to see because they just might.

If she has posted something cool or interesting, or a statement you agree with, like the tweet and re-tweet them.

On Friday, put together a list of people and do a #followfriday Tweet that includes them.

Facebook

Facebook is a bit different because you need to friend someone before you can really communicate. So, you need to know them or their friends before you can start anything.

If they are friends of a friend, send them a friend request with a note that mentions your connection. If it's someone you have no connection with, I would be careful about sending out blind friend requests. They can report you for that, and too many offenses will get you banned from Facebook.

Look for mutual friends and a photo that features someone you know. Like their photo and then consider sending a friend request. After the friend request goes through, send her a short message just to say hi and that it was great meeting her or however it went down.

After you become Facebook friends, post things on her page that she likes and to which she has a connection. Do you know she has a dog? Post a cute puppy photo or video on her page with a simple note "Reminded me of you."

Don't overdo it. Don't post too much or make too many comments or likes. It can be a fine line between flirty and stalker, so go with the idea of less is more. Start a conversation chain.

Use messenger to send them a message but make sure there's a reason for the contact. Even if it shows that they are online, it's doesn't go ever well to just go "Hey whatcha up to?"

Make a connection. Did she post a photo that you liked? Then find a connection with it. Maybe they posted a picture of Chicago and you were born there. Mention that.

Keep the conversation going. Answer her questions and then wait for her reply. Send another question based on her reply. Engage her.

Take it offline. Don't drive the online flirtation on forever. Suggest that you should get together in person for coffee or drinks.

Dating Apps

Ah... dating apps. After millennia of men needing to go out hunting for opportunities to meet women, technology has brought the hunt right to your fingertips.

Now you can swipe left, meet women and flirt without ever leaving the comfort of your own couch. But are the rules different? Do you need to approach it differently?

The first thing you need to understand is that, and it's probably pretty obvious, women are on dating sites and apps because they want to meet men. Unlike a bar, women are going to create a profile to meet someone. If they are in a bar or restaurant, they may just want to have a drink or food and could already be in a relationship or just not looking.

So, this means that you have an opportunity to work on your flirting skills with someone who is actually open to them.

Most of the apps work the same, by selecting people that you find attractive and interesting. Once matches are made, they give you the opportunity to interact, but each app has its own way of doing it. Some apps charge to unlock some features while others may require you to pay for even basic communication.

Be aware of bots and scams on apps, just like other dating sites.

Also, be careful of becoming a serial dater on the apps. I once went out with a few girls on some of the apps, and it turned out that they talked to each other online. They explained that while the girls had nothing but good things to say about me, there were other men on the apps that they exchanged information on frequently.

Which App Should I Try?

It seems like every day there is a new app out there for dating, but there are less than a half dozen that have become the most successful way to meet and flirt. Here are some of the most popular ones:

Tinder

Probably the most popular of all dating apps, Tinder claims to have over 50 million active users and created the now ubiquitous "swipe left/swipe right" that is now the norm for most dating apps. It's become a worldwide phenomenon being used in over 140 countries and 30 languages.

You are limited to a certain number of swipes per day unless you pay for a membership. Also, purchasing a membership can get you special perks like looking for people in different areas, undo swipes and "superlikes", which theoretically get you more notice.

Bumble

This app has become more and more popular due to the way it gives the power to women. When two people match, the app requires women to message you first, and if you don't reply within 24 hours, you lose the match.

Bumble also features friendship and business networking sections. With a paid membership you receive many of the same types of perks as Tinder.

Bumble tends to skew a bit older, and most women say they are looking for serious relationships, but there are definitely women of all ages looking for various connections.

Happn

This is an interesting app because while other apps tell you who is nearby, this tells you who just almost met. Using your phone's GPS capabilities, it tells you who you have been in close proximity to. You might have almost met a cute girl at your coffee shop and didn't even know it. Well, now you can write and talk to her.

The app doesn't tell you right away, so it helps eliminate any creep or stalking factors. It's a great way to find common interests or activities and start a conversation and flirtation with the information.

Plenty of Fish

Like Match.com and other dating site-based apps, this is more about finding a date. Like the aforementioned sites, most are going to require you to pay before you can find any meaningful interaction.

Email

Email is simply the modern way of sending notes or what used to be called love letters. It requires a bit more writing finesse and some expert flirting but is by no means impossible.

- Don't forget that compliments and innuendo work in emails, too.

- Leave them wondering. Write things that will have them asking questions and writing back. Drop breadcrumbs about an interesting thing that happened to you that they will want to read more.

- Don't write a book. It's longer than a text, but you don't need to write thousands of words to them. And always remember to use paragraph breaks.

- Always double-check who you are emailing. Make sure you have the right address and no accidental CCs of BCCs. You don't accidentally want to send a sexy email to your mom!

Chapter 9: Restaurants, Bars and Nightclubs

Probably the most common places to meet women is when you go out with your friends or even by yourself. Usually, people end up in a bar or restaurant, and there are special ways to approach people in those locations.

I already discussed some of the basics about how to approach women, which applies to most places, not just bars and clubs and the like. But here are a few more specifics.

Dancing

Some guys think the best way to approach a girl at a loud club is just to start grinding. Either she'll be into it, or she'll walk away.

No. Don't do this.

To begin, it's just really without class, not to mention that depending on how you do it, it could honestly be mistaken for attempted sexual assault. And we haven't even gotten to her MMA cage-fighting boyfriend who has been watching the entire time. Even if she's not with a big boyfriend or an equally big male friend or relative, she is most likely there with one or more female friends. Women stick together, especially on a night out, and will make sure that everyone in their group feels safe while having fun. So, save the possible slap, arrest or major butt-whooping and act like a man.

Catch her eye, nod along to the music and smile. Gently rock back and forth while maintaining eye contact. Don't break out some dance move, just move slightly to the music. Most of the time, she'll invite you over to dance with her.

Watch the Pickup Lines

We've already gone over this, so by now you should know that legitimate conversation will always get your farther than some cheesy pickup line. Remember that you are in a place where she has already probably been hit on a half dozen or more times before you even saw her.

Be genuine. Also, realize a lot of the time you are not going to be able to have a deep conversation in a loud club. Look for the opportunities to talk to her near the bar or other places where the music might not be so distracting.

Bear in mind that clubs are noisy and might require you to shout or lean in really close. This can backfire as you might make your potential target uncomfortable. If possible, find a less noisy location. Of course, if that is not possible, hand gestures work rather well. The main thing to avoid is moving in too close as this may trigger a defensive response.

Sending Over Drinks

I'm not a fan of this. If you like someone and want to buy them a drink, go over and talk to them. All buying a round of drinks for their table does is show that you are trying to buy their interest with money and alcohol. Personally, I believe that you are merely throwing your cash away.

By walking over and having a drink with a woman personally, you get to have a few minutes to talk while you sip. I know so many women who go to bars with the intent of trying to get free drinks merely for how they look. Don't buy in and perpetuate this type of behavior.

Although, bear in mind that some women will shy away from accepting drinks from strangers, even when it is well-intentioned, as they may be concerned about something being slipped into the drinks. Since this is unfortunately common, you might want to make sure that you establish some type of eye contact first before attempting to try this.

If you notice a woman doing something like dipping her fingernail into the drink you bought her before trying it, she's probably testing it for date rape drugs. In recent years, some devices have been invented in order to help women identify when something has been slipped into their drinks, including nail polish that changes color if certain drugs are present. Don't take offense to this. It's nothing against you personally. Let her do whatever makes her feel more comfortable, and soon she'll see that she can at least trust you enough to drink and chat with you. If not, it's best for the both of you if you just move on.

How to Flirt with Waitresses and Bartenders

The first thing you need to know is that female bartenders and waitresses flirt for a living. So, you need to be careful that what you think is reciprocation isn't just them angling for a bigger tip.

Waitresses and bartenders love confidence, but not overconfidence. Talking yourself up and throwing money around isn't going to get them to give you their number. In fact, a lot of female bartenders will actually use this as an excuse to get you to come back in, hang out and spend more money.

I've personally dated a number of waitresses and bartenders, and what I quickly realized is that they have two different styles of flirtation. First, they have the one that they use with you, the guy they are dating. This is their real personality, the one you see when they aren't at work.

Then they have their "act" that they put on at work. While they may be very similar, you can tell the difference.

Always pay attention to their eyes. If you learn the signs, you can tell the difference between a smile to get a bigger tip and a smile with a twinkle in the eyes which is the sign of legitimate interest in you.

Don't try the small talk route, either. Don't comment on their looks or outfit. This might actually backfire. Remember that they often are dressing or looking a certain way for work, so complimenting that just means that their look is working. Remember, they hear those compliments dozens of times every shift, and they use them to make bigger tips.

Look for ways to compliment and talk about her personality and interests. Get her to talk about life outside of the bar or restaurant.

Always remember, **they are working**. They are on the clock and making money, so don't dominate their time. However, if you notice they are spending a lot of time talking to you and not all their customers, it's a good sign.

When you offer them your number, don't hang around after. Give it to them, smile and leave. They have a lot on their mind.

Let them come to you. If a waitress or bartender is on a break, remember that it's their break. This may be the only ten minutes they get all night to rest or eat. Interrupting that is not going to endear you to them.

If you frequent a bar and there is a waitress or bartender you are interested in, try to come in on a slower night when they will have time to talk. You are going to have to do a small amount of investigation for this and make sure you do it without the creep factor. Ask her or her coworkers nonchalantly what nights during the week they work. Follow up with a question about what nights are slow. But be cool!

When you do visit on a slower night, still don't try to dominate her time. See if she talks to you and be pleasant when she does. By the time you get ready to leave, you'll know if she's interested. However, if she's not, don't keep coming back or you might start to make her uncomfortable. She'll still be nice because it's her job, but any chance of getting her number will be long gone.

And if you start to be inappropriate, always remember that the bouncers at bars are usually really big and very experienced at tossing guys out onto the street.

Chapter 10: At Work

Let's start this one with a disclaimer- BE VERY CAREFUL FLIRTING AT WORK!

While it is true, many people have found the loves of their lives there (as well as a few fun flings), flirting and dating at the office can be very dangerous. There may be actual regulations against dating; you most likely have a very detailed sexual harassment handbook at work.

If it goes wrong, the best-case scenario is an uncomfortable work environment, while the worst-case scenario is that you could be suspended, reprimanded or even lose your job. It doesn't even have to be something you did. All too often, the most innocent flirting can be misinterpreted and cause huge work-related issues.

Always keep it light and joking and always be appropriate. In the beginning, never venture into the area of sex or of an inappropriate nature. Never comment on their body, sexual acts or anything in this area. Also, never touch your coworkers. In many companies, these are not just good things to abide by, they are literally against the rules and could get you fired.

Obvious Is a Safe Zone

A new hairstyle or outfit is a great way to flirt by paying a compliment. It's something everyone can see and something that the woman is most likely happy about and would love the compliment.

But, as always, watch the creep factor. Don't leer, don't give her some innuendo about how she looks or what you would like to do to her. Just pay her a sincere, honest compliment.

Be careful about complimenting her about non-tangible things like personality. It's one thing to say she has a great sense of humor, but be careful of delving into personality traits that might sound more invasive of her private life.

Drinking and Coworkers

Be very careful when drinking is involved. Over the last few years, more and more companies have done away with the traditional holiday party due to tightening budgets but also because they are trying to avoid possible scenarios for inappropriate sexual situations. However, there are still after-work events, mixers and the like.

Be careful and make sure that you are always in control. It may be a fun time and could even lead to more, but the next day at work could be very awkward.

You can be very successful with her because you are away from the confines of work. Just use the tips we have already discussed to push the flirtation forward.

You Are Your Own Best Judge

If you commented and you feel strange about it after, it's a pretty good sign that you went too far. You may want to find the appropriate way to apologize but keep it simple. Don't make the situation worse. If it was really bad, you might receive a visit from your human resources office. Take responsibility for what you said; be contrite and honest.

Be very observant of her reactions from the first flirt. If she looks uncomfortable or shocked, this is a sign you need to stop. If she responds back, it's a sign you are ok. Be cool. If you realize that your flirting isn't welcome, don't make it weird. Continue talking and being pleasant. You still need to work together.

Also, be aware she may not flirt back immediately. It might be a few hours or days before she responds. Don't make it weird in the meantime by hovering, annoying her or making a big deal about it. Be cool, and women will respond to it.

As the flirtation progresses and intensifies, you'll be able to up the intensity. But always be aware of her reactions. Also, make sure it doesn't get to the point that you are beginning to be noticed by others in the office. This could lead to work issues or a visit from human resources.

It could even happen that she's into you but tells you that work is not the place where she feels comfortable interacting like that. That's not a bad thing. She's into it, but you just need to adjust your approach.

Find Commonalities

Use your work experience as a flirt starter. Talk about a rough project you are working on or an upcoming deadline. Maybe talk about how you might react in certain situations.

Maybe even play some "What if" games. Joke with her what it might be like if the two of you ran the company or something silly like what if you sold candy instead of copy machine parts at the business. Keep it fun and make her laugh and you are on track.

Don't Spread It Around

There are some people, men and women, who just love to flirt. It's part of their personality, and they spread it around. They'll flirt with coworkers, friends, the barista or a random woman on the street. Basically, everyone they interact with on a daily basis.

However, most people aren't like this, and a lot of times people who do are looked at negatively.

So, be careful flirting with everyone at work. If there is someone you are specifically interested in, you are going to be far more successful if they know they are the only one you are flirting with. If they know you flirt with everyone in the office, they aren't going to take you seriously, and you may even be labeled as the office flirt or worse.

Chapter 11: With Neighbors

Rom-coms and romance novels are filled with men and women flirting with their new neighbors, eventually winning them over and living happily ever after, but is it really a good idea? Like with flirting at work, it's a social gray area.

So, once again: BE CAREFUL.

Flirting gone awry at work could lead to sexual harassment complaints and possible loss of job. For the most part, though, you'll have a haven from the debacle at your own home. If you flirt with a neighbor and it goes wrong, though, not only can it go horrifically south, but it will always be there staring you in the face.

It's not that you need to avoid it altogether. In fact, most people are probably guilty of flirting with a neighbor for some harmless fun, like when flirting with a cashier at the check-out line. Still, you need to be more careful how you do it.

Better Safe than Sorry

Earlier, I talked about how a little flirting with a married woman just for fun is okay so long as you don't overstep your bounds. The same applies here, but even more caution might called for.

Neighborhoods, whether they be made of traditional houses or they're just an apartment building, are notorious for gossip that spreads like wildfire. If you're caught in even some harmless flirting with a married neighbor, word will get around and it will probably not end well for either of you.

Practice Makes Perfect

That being said, your female neighbors can also be the perfect people to practice your flirting skills on. If you aren't that close to them, seeing if you can turn on the charm and captivate them—or at least get them to have a little fun—can really help you gauge your abilities. If you usually get the feeling that they don't like you, all the better. If you can get Ms. Landry in 3B who hates your guts to crack a smile, you should have no problem with the more laid-back woman nursing a beer up at the bar.

The best time to give your flirting muscles a workout are at neighborhoods gatherings, like a BBQ, a potluck, or a block party. You'll have your pick of the bunch, and any of them are married, their spouses will most likely be there to see that no harm is meant, as well as multiple witnesses.

New Neighbor

Ah, yes, the Hallmark/Lifetime fantasy of finding love with the new neighbor. It's a bit cheesy, but anything's possible. With their close proximity, there should be plenty of opportunities to flirt with the new girl next door. The trick is doing it without coming off as a creep.

Housewarming Gift

It might seem like a sitcom cliché, but a housewarming gift would be the perfect chance to introduce yourself to your new neighbor. You'll get to chat her up a bit, and she might even invite you into the house for a cup of coffee if she feels that you aren't too threatening.

Make sure that the gift you bring is something unique, not some store-bought cookies or a potted plant. Give her something that would be appreciated by someone who's just moving in, like some real homecooked food or some artwork for the walls. Use it as your chance to break the ice with her and maybe show off one of your talents, like cooking, baking, or painting.

And mind the hours when you come to drop the gift off. Make sure that it's an appropriate time for visitors, not too early and not too late. Otherwise, she might be turned off by you being so overeager if you come too early or by you seeming like a creep if you drop by too late.

Offer to Help

Do you know how to put together furniture or set up WiFi? Are you a particularly good handyman or willing to help put things away? Offer to help your new neighbor get settled in. This will give you an excuse to spend more time with her in her house and provide more opportunities for non-verbal flirting. You can subtly touch her hand as she hands you a box, you can show off your physique as you stretch to put the last book on the top shelf, and you can even play around a bit, dancing to whatever music she has put on her playlist since the TV hasn't been hooked up yet.

Your help doesn't have to be limited to household work, either. Offer to give her a tour of the neighborhood or the city. Take her to your favorite lunch spot or show her the best dog park. Act like you're letting her in on the secrets of your city and your neighborhood, and she'll enjoy it as such.

The Mail Meet Up

This one is fairly cliché. So cliché, in fact, that it has been made fun of multiple times on sitcoms like *The Big Bang Theory*. However, that doesn't mean it doesn't work.

I'm not talking about stealing your new neighbor's mail just as an excuse to talk to her. However, everyone has to check their mail eventually. Why not make sure that you check yours at a time when you can bump into her? Don't necessarily try and brush it off as an accident—women will often see through that—but use it as a springboard for your flirtation.

Don't Be a Stalker

Part of the problem with flirting with a neighbor is knowing where exactly to draw the line. After all, you both live in the same neighborhood. You'll probably be seeing her a lot, so be careful about going out of your way to see her. There's a fine line between flirting and stalking.

Chapter 12: Unconventional Settings

So far in this book, we've looked into the more obvious places to flirt, both physical and virtual locations. But what about those places that aren't so obvious, ones that aren't off limits but that people still don't typically think of?

Depending on where you live, the go-to settings might not be the best places to flirt. In some cases, they aren't even available. Rural areas might have some bars and restaurants, but other than that, the usual choices are few and far between. Even in cities, a lot of restaurants, bars, and clubs could be bad places to flirt due to the kinds of people—the kinds of women—they attract. That's when some creativity is needed.

Farmer's Markets

Are you a food or health nut? Then the local farmer's market might be the perfect place for you to flirt with women. There are plenty of women to consider, from other customers to women running or working at booths, and plenty of opportunities for both verbal and non-verbal flirtation. It is also an open space operating in broad daylight, which means that women will feel safer and are less likely to think that you're a creep so long as you don't do or say something creepy.

Now, a farmer's market is not exactly a place where women would expect to be hit on, so there aren't the exact same moves that can be used at places like bars and clubs. Some are similar, yes, but not all the tricks of the club will work here. Instead, you'll have to get a bit more creative with your flirting, but they are there.

With female vendors, providing genuine compliments about their products can be a great start. You might strike up a conversation about how good the food looks and suggest that you might have to come by their booth more often. Slip some subtle innuendo and double meanings in there, but do not, ever, slip in a joke about their "melons". I guarantee you that they have heard those a million times before, even if the people weren't flirting with them.

When flirting with other customers, make use of the fact that you're in a place you're familiar with. Ask them if they've been to a certain booth or tried certain produce. If it's their first time there, offer to show them around to your favorite booths and where they can get the best of the best.

And don't forget to show off *your* wares. Brush your hand against hers as you show hand her an apple. Stretch up and grab her that watermelon from the top of the stack and offer to carry it for her if it's too heavy. Most importantly, remember to wear something nice and fitting. As this is a more casual gathering place, a clean white shirt and a pair of jeans will do wonders for showing your assets off, and you'll look right at home in the more agricultural setting.

Tourist Hot Spots

Except for the most rural of areas, everywhere has at least one tourist hot spot: museums, modern art installations, historic landmarks, national parks, etc. They are also great places to meet and flirt with women. You have a built-in topic of interest with the hot spot itself, and women will be eager to learn anything they can about it from a local like you.

There's also a unique advantage to flirting with women who are just coming through on vacation. You know the phrase "What happens in Vegas, stays in Vegas"? The same is true for most vacations. The women who come to these tourist hot spots are just looking to have some fun and relax, and that might make them a little more open to some flirting. There's even a bit of an adventurous element to flirting with a total stranger on a road trip, so long as they feel safe. Just remember that this also means that they might be less likely to look to you for anything serious, but it still makes for great practice.

If you do hit it off while flirting with a woman at a tourist hot spot, it's more important than ever to get her phone number. Otherwise, you might never see them again.

Meetup.com

Earlier in the book, I talk about using meetups to meet new women. Meetup.com is a site where you can do just that: find people in your area with the same interests as you and meet up as a group to discuss/participate in these interests. You can find groups for almost any interest on there, from photography and art to outdoor adventures and food. All you have to do is join the site, look for a group or groups you're interested in, and get to know some new people.

Meetup.com is an interesting blend of online and in-person flirting. You first talk to the people you'll meet up with online, discussing your common likes and goals with the possibility—and the probability—of meeting in person somewhere in your city. Then you get to meet in a group setting that, while less intimate, is also less intimidating for women.

With places like Meetup.com, you have a two-fold advantage: guaranteed common ground with the woman you're flirting with and a topic you're knowledgeable about. Those combined will give you plenty of ammunition and maybe an excuse for the two of you to get together again after the meeting—alone.

Chapter 13: How to Flirt with Older Women

There are many names for them. MILFs, Cougars, even GILFs (if you don't know that one, look it up). However you care to describe them, older women are amazing to spend time with. They have life experience, are incredibly interesting to talk with and spend time with and are absolutely beautiful. And the sex is always spectacular.

When I was just out of college, I dated a gorgeous older woman in her early 40s named Miriam. I learned a lot from her about life, women, and sex. Her experience and outlook helped me grow from a horny, fresh college graduate to a man who understood the physical and emotional needs of women.

While every woman is obviously different, we can break older women into two main categories.

The first are women who are looking for a boy toy and maybe even want to spoil them a bit. It's not just about sex and physical attraction, but that's a lot of it. Women in this category might also want to show you off a little bit. They will buy you gifts, jewelry, and clothing as well as take you to events and parties. There might even be some aspects of wanting to nurture and take care of you.

The second group are women looking for something a bit more meaningful but want it with a younger, sexy man like you.

For some women, the label of cougar is negative, while others embrace it and find it very fulfilling. No matter how attractive a woman may already be, having a younger man find them attractive, sexy and vivacious is always going to be a turn on even if they don't outwardly admit it.

Another great thing about flirting with older women is that they enjoy it and are usually pretty good at it. Often, older women will play more with innuendo and be forward with what they like and don't like.

Why Older Women Are Special

They Know What They Want

Older women have experience. I'm not just talking about sex. I mean in the world and life. And this usually means they know what they want and go after it.

They don't like to play games, but they still like the game of dating. They enjoy flirting as much as anyone else and sometimes can be very upfront about their needs and desires.

You're Going to Learn from Them

Again, I'm not just talking about sex. They have more experience. They have knowledge about the world, current events, dating, and a myriad of other subjects.

They Are Secure

Older women are much more secure in their personality and appearance. While they may be a little sensitive about the random gray hair or wrinkle, their life experience grounds them in a way they aren't going to become unpredictable.

They Aren't All About Appearances

Older women know that there is more to a book than its cover. They know that attraction is not only physical but what's in your brain as well.

They Have Cultivated Tastes

Older women have had time to not only learn what they enjoy when it comes to film, food, art, and other subjects, but they've also had the time to explore it and learn more about their interests. If they are into a certain author, they have had time to read all of their work. Or if there is a painter they enjoy, it's because they have a life of memories and exposure.

They are going to be able to open you up to a world of culture and knowledge you could never imagine. And again, not just talking about sex!

Also, they aren't going to spend their night trying to post selfies and create some sort of social media impression. They are much happier snuggling in a corner booth over a drink and talking.

Where to Meet Older Women

It's not difficult to meet women of any age. I happened to meet Miriam through one of her coworkers, a vet tech and female friend/neighbor of mine that I mentioned in ***How to Talk to Women***. Just because they are older doesn't make them harder to find, but there are a few places where you might have a better opportunity to start up a flirty conversation.

Classes

No, not in school, we aren't talking about your teacher (although don't discount the opportunity if it arises). We mean like adult education classes such as cooking, art, business prep or other classes. It's actually a great way to meet women in general, but there is a larger percentage of attractive older women who take these classes.

Bookstores

Bookstores are a great place to meet cultured and well-read women of any age, and many older women like to read. Meeting women here works best if you're already an avid reader, but so long as you have a couple of books that you liked well enough to discuss, you should be able to start something. You could even use your lack of reading as an excuse to ask an attractive older woman for some suggestions on where to start in a certain genre or for a certain author.

Your greatest chances of success will come if you stick with genres that you're interested in. There might be more attractive older women checking out the romance section, but if war stories are more your thing, you'll run out of things to talk about quickly, and soon you'll be left with nothing but rows of shirtless Fabios staring at you.

Dog Parks

A lot of older women have dogs or other pets. Now, while you may want to be a bit wary of the woman who is covered in cat hair, women who have dogs are usually independent, smart and outgoing. They are usually more secure and ready to have some fun.

Don't lie to them and bring your friend's dog and pretend it's yours. Be honest. If it's yours, say so, if it's a friend's, say so, but it's a great way to strike up a conversation and open up some flirting.

Don't adopt a dog or other pet just to meet women, either. This isn't fair to the woman, the pet, or you. A pet is a lifetime commitment and deserves your love for longer than it takes to snag a woman's attention. Not to mention how much a woman will hate you if she finds out that that's the only reason you adopted an animal and how immature older women will find you as a result.

Bars

Bars can be a good place to meet older women. Consider bars at restaurants without loud music but be careful.

Cougars and MILFs often have a lot of life pressures and time commitments. Could be job or kids, but they don't usually frequent bars a few times a week like their younger counterparts. If they are going to a bar, it's usually to relax and because they are open to meeting someone like you.

However, as you talk to them, make sure that you aren't talking to the woman who is in that bar every night on the same barstool. You might just end up buying drinks all night and going home without even a number.

The Gym

This is great because you have a chance to meet women who take care of themselves and you already have a common interest. If you offer to assist with a workout issue, make sure you know what you are talking about. I see guys walk up to girls all the time trying to explain stuff that the woman didn't want to know. I even see out-of-shape men try to flirt with women in way better shape than them by explaining how to do the exercise they are already doing correctly. It's actually embarrassing to watch as a man.

Volunteering

Right from the start, volunteering is just a great thing to do. You should be doing it just to be a good human being. But it's also a great place to meet older women.

When older women have extra time, they love to give back. You can give your time as well and be able to get to know them and show that you have some qualities that they find very attractive as you help others.

Hiking and Jogging

Where I live, we have a large number of trails where people go to get their workouts, and many of these people are very attractive older women who like to get outdoors and get some active exercise.

This is a great place to meet and talk to people. Easy conversation starters about the trail, the weather, the hiking difficulty can lead to bigger conversations and great opening s for flirting and getting to know each other.

Church

I will admit this one isn't for everyone. If you are religious, then it might be a good place to meet older women. However, you will want to be very careful with your flirting. It could go down the wrong path quite quickly, and you might be ostracized from your place of worship.

Conversations with Older Women

If you want to have a conversation with an older woman, she is definitely not going to want to hear about your high score on X-Box or how many beers you downed last night. On the other hand, she probably doesn't want to hear your thoughts on the Middle East peace process.

That woman is going to want to have a conversation with someone with opinions and knowledge. So, make sure you come in having done your homework. Know a little bit about a lot of things.

And if you don't know about something that she does, use that. Remember how we talked about listening? This is a great place to use that skill.

Let her explain a concept to you or something from her work or life. Listen to her and ask questions. This will make her feel appreciated and that she is valuable for her knowledge without having her feel older because of it.

Her Age

Don't make it an issue, but don't pretend it's not there. If she brings it up, make comments that you don't see it or you never would have guessed. If she comes out and asks you to guess her age, always temper your guess by a few years downward. Don't be an idiot, though. Don't throw out a number half her age to try to be cute.

Just be careful about comments that might make her feel that she's out of touch. Don't say things like "that was way before my time," or "I had only heard about those from my mother/father/parents."

Her Past

Experience and wisdom can sometimes come with loose threads. Just like you shouldn't dig too deeply too quickly with younger women, you shouldn't pry too much into an older woman's earlier years unless she offers information up first. She might not be ready to talk about it, or she might not want to talk about it unless she's sure that this is anything more than just a flirtation or a one-night stand.

There are some things that might come up in an older woman's past that are less likely to appear with younger women. While this can be trauma or something similarly tragic, they aren't always bad. The most common remnant of an older woman's past is usually a child or children from a previous relationship. You might panic at the very thought of this, but you shouldn't necessarily reject older women for this reason alone.

Miriam told me about her children on our third date. Internally, I freaked out a bit, thinking about how I was barely more than a kid myself and that it was so early in the relationship, I could probably just bail and there'd be no hard feelings. There was something about Miriam, though, and so I decided to stick it out. I met her children, a pair of pre-teen boys, and we hit it off. Even though they spent every other week at their dad's place across town, I really got to like Miriam's sons. Even after the relationship ended, we still greeted each other warmly whenever we saw each other at the mall or the park. Knowing them even helped me get over my fear of having children.

If an older woman tells you that she has children early in the conversation, there could be a number of reasons. She might not want to blindside you with the truth later if your relationship blossoms.

Miriam told me that's why she told me about her children with her ex-husband on our third date even though she had been too nervous to tell me during the first two. An older woman might also have had experience with men, both younger and their own age, having problems accepting that she has children and just wants to get it out of the way. Conversely, an older woman might decide to wait to tell you to avoid scaring you off.

Whether she brings it up in your first conversation or on your twentieth date, it's best to let the older woman bring up the topic of her children if and when she's ready. If she does bring it up, don't make a big deal of it. Don't hide if you don't like children—honesty is the best policy—but don't be rude about it, either. Say something like "Oh, kids aren't really my thing", thank her for her time and move on or tell her that you'd be willing to meet them if the time ever comes.

Nothing huge, no commitments, and no big fuss. Remember, flirting is supposed to be fun.

Play the Confidence and Independence Cards

We've already hit it before how much confidence plays into flirting and talking to women, but it's a different type with older women.

Most older women want a man who is independent and confident. While they like your youthful exuberance (and body), they don't want to hear about your roommates, video games or how you are probably going to be late on the rent this month.

Boy Toy

I touched on this a bit earlier. Just like many older men like to have a younger woman on their arm, some older women want the same thing with their own personal boy toy.

This may or may not be for you. It also depends on what you are looking for. If you are looking for a fun time with very few strings attached, then here you go.

However, just like the older man with the younger woman who is just about looks, you may not have much to talk about. If you are looking for a meaningful relationship, you're going to need to bring more to the table and also make sure that's what she is looking for. Quite often, a woman older than you is just looking to have a good time.

Chapter 14: How to Flirt While Travelling

Whether you are on a plane or waiting in a terminal or other form of travel, it's a great place to strike up conversations and flirt a bit.

While the Holy Grail is to be seated next to an amazing woman on the plane and you talk to each other the entire flight and exchange numbers, it doesn't always happen. So, you might need to be a bit more creative.

Try an App

Earlier I mentioned several apps, including one called Happn. Try this while you're in the airport, especially if you have a layover or long wait before your flight.

Happn will actually show you who is around the terminal. You might be able to use it to strike up a fun conversation with a nice female traveler also waiting for their flight. It's also a great way to meet flight attendants who are in the terminal and looking for some conversation.

You can do this with apps like Tinder as well, but those don't give you the actual geographic location like Happn does. After a few minutes of safety buffer, the app will actually show you the location where you almost ran into each other down to a few feet. If you both make a connection (swipe on each other) you can then agree to meet back where you almost met.

Flight Attendants

Ah, the female bartenders of the sky.

Now, I don't mean this as a demeaning comment in any way. Flight attendants work very hard, put up with a lot of annoying travelers and have a lot to deal with. I mean it in the way that if you are going to try to flirt with them, they are just like bartenders. They are working, have a lot on their mind, and it probably happens to them several dozen times a day that some guy thinks he can sweep them off their feet.

- Many flight attendants wear nametags. If not, ask politely. Use her name when speaking to her, but don't do it creepily. Smile when you say her name, it'll go a long way to making her like you.

- Try asking a legitimate question about the flight or the arrival airport, but make sure it's something she will either know the answer for or can easily find out. Don't ask her anything stupid or that is going to be a waste of her time. Try to pose a question that can open up a chance to talk, like if she has ever spent time in the destination you are going to and can recommend places to eat or do things.

- Get to know her. Ask her real questions. Flight attendants are people just like you, and they have a life outside of work. It's a common problem that men too often just think of them as their employment, similar to a waitress or bartender. You wouldn't just want to talk about your job, would you?

- Don't mention the Mile-High Club. They have heard all the jokes, and most likely it will end the conversation then and there. If you decide to go there, it better be the most clever, funny or sly comment that flight attendant has ever heard.

- Listen for codes and cues. Flight attendants have their own language they use, so passengers don't know what they are talking about. Sometimes they will reveal who they are talking about with cues like your seat number, but they might put it with a country. Something like "I'm interested in going to Canada in six days." If you are in seat 6C and they are looking your way, they might be talking about you.

- International flights are always going to be a better opportunity. While the attendants still have their duties, a longer amount of time in the air means they have more opportunities to talk and chat.

- Offer to help when appropriate. When you are getting on a plane, look for the chance to set yourself apart in a good way. Smile and be friendly. Not just to the crew, but other passengers. If someone is having dif-

ficulty getting their luggage into the over-
head compartment, lend a hand. Offer to
stand up to let people pass instead of making them crawl over you. These things get
noticed by flight attendants and will do
wonders for how they view you.

- Start small. Don't launch into a big conversation right as the plane is getting ready to
take off. Offer brief, witty comments and
jokes. Keep it light and fun.

- Be polite. Say please and thank you.

- Don't compliment her on her uniform. And
stay away from the usual questions about
liking her job or it must be fun to travel.
She's heard them thousands of times.

- Always remember, she is working. So, if
she gets called away or is doing something
while you are trying to talk, that's your cue
to go back to your seat. If she's interested,
she'll come by your seat, and you'll know.

- A trick I learned from a flight attendant ac-
quaintance of mine is always put your
shoes on when you go to the bathroom.
Other than the ick factor, it also shows
them that you are courteous of others.

Plus, who wants to step in something in socks in the lavatory? Eww.

- Look for a real opportunity. If she says she has a layover at your airport, invite her for a drink before you head out. Make sure it's going to fit into her schedule because flight attendants can be very busy, but they also can have long stretches of unused time.

- Don't ask for her number. Give her yours. And don't do it until the end of the flight or when it seems appropriate...especially if she asked you for it.

- Don't call then stewardess. This was a term commonly used in the past, but now it is seen as a derogatory term in this profession and can even go against their personal virtue. It is seen as demeaning them to just being eye candy, even though their job is much more important than that today. It is much better to ask them their names and call them by that.

Look for the Signs She's Interested:

- You are getting a lot of attention. We know that's a flight attendant's job, but you can tell when she is spending way more time checking in on your needs.

- Compare how she treats you to others around you. If she seems to ignore them, including your own seatmate, something might be up.

- If you get offered extra drinks or are just given one, this is a sign you are more than just an average passenger to them.

- Random upgrades. Sometimes it happens, they'll just come up and ask you to gather your things so they can put you in first class. It has happened to me a few times.

One last note: if she hands you a napkin, always check it before throwing it away. I've actually seen beautiful flight attendants slip their number to guys and they didn't even realize it was on the napkin!

Flirting with the Locals

When you are travelling in foreign countries, it doesn't mean that you can't flirt. In fact, it's an excellent opportunity. Many women in other countries love American men and love to talk to them.

Learn a Few Words in the Local Language

You don't have to become proficient but learn a few handy phrases like "Hello" and "Thank you" and maybe learn something flirty like "You have beautiful hair."

Be Careful What You Are Dealing With

In some countries, being American automatically means you have money. In other places, the women will see you as a ticket to America. Be careful of being taken advantage of, either emotionally or criminally.

Use Your Uniqueness

Especially in Asia, an American is exotic just by sight. Being tall, whenever I visit Asia, I am always the center of attention. I had an African American friend who I was with who women would always want to touch his hair.

In other countries, once you say a few words, it's going to be obvious you aren't a local. Use this! You know how women in America go crazy over foreign men? Well, now it's your turn to be the unique one and get all that attention.

Be Observant

Always know where your wallet and passport are and never allow anyone else to have them.

Also, in certain countries in Asia, be aware that the girl you are talking to might actually be a very feminine guy. Plus be very aware of overly friendly women that might be prostitutes. You don't want to end up in jail in another country, get robbed or worse.

Body Language

This is different in every country. Trust me.

A few years ago, I travelled to Russia for business. While I was there, I was lucky enough to have a lovely young woman who was my guide and translator. So, she was able to explain to me how people perceived me and my actions.

One of the things I did was smile at people, especially women. However, I didn't get the response that I expected. People would look at me strangely and rarely return the smile. I finally asked my guide, and the answer was very shocking.

In Russia, people don't smile that much publicly. In the United States, we use it as a non-verbal greeting. We will walk down the street and smile at passersby. But in Russia, they don't believe in smiling unless you are genuinely happy about something or talking with someone. To Russians, it's almost as if there are only so many smiles to go around, so they save them up.

I asked my guide what people thought of me when I smiled at strangers. She giggled and tried to find the right English words. "They think you are crazy in the head," she explained to me, and we both laughed.

So, make sure you know some things about the local customs and body language.

Here are a few examples:

- **Albania**- Yes and no, in terms of the gesture, are opposite. Shaking your head means yes and nodding it means no.

- **Japan**- Eye contact can be seen as uncomfortable. Broad gesturing with your hands and arms is also considered rude.

- **Muslim Countries**- Using your left hand for actions such as eating is frowned upon. It's also considered very rude to cross your legs and point the soul of your shoe at a person.

- **Thailand**- It's considered impolite to touch people's heads. It's also rude to point.

- **India**- Public displays of affection are frowned upon. Also, the American hand-wave hello is seen to them as "go away."

- **Argentina, Cuba, and Brazil**- The classic heavy metal pinky and index finger exposed (also the longhorn symbol) means something completely different in these countries. It actually is a signal to tell someone their significant other is cheating on them.

- **Britain**- If you make the peace sign with two fingers, but the back of your hand is toward a person, it means that you are telling them to $%# off.

- **Korea**- Keeping your hands in your pockets is considered a sign of arrogance.

- **Greece**- If you playfully put your hand up in the "Talk to the hand" position, you are actually telling them something similar to "I'm going to rub feces in your face."

- **East Africa**- The "thumbs up" sign actually means "Up Yours."

One Last Reminder Before Conclusion

Have you grabbed your free resource?

A lot of information has been covered in this book. As previously shared, I've created a simple mind map that you can use _right away_ to easily understand, quickly recall and readily use what you've learned in this book.

If you've not grabbed it...

Click Here To Get Your Free Resource

Alternatively, here's the link:

https://viebooks.club/freeresourcemindmapfor-howtoflirtwithwomen

Conclusion

In this book, I laid out some very specific ways that you can change your approach to flirting, but always remember that the most important things are confidence and listening.

If you believe in yourself, that inner confidence will read to others. Not just women, but everyone you interact with.

As for your listening skills, remember how important they are. It's how you can stay in a power position when flirting, by continually tweaking your game based on the information you receive. Again, like confidence, it will help you in all stages of your life.

With these skills and a healthy dose of respect for the opposite sex, you are well on your way to successful flirting and conversation!

I urge you to pick up my books ***How to Talk to Women*** and ***How to Attract Women***. I go into much deeper detail on how to have conversations, breaking the ice, and getting and going on that first date. I also delve into some of the mindset issues you are probably dealing with that are keeping you from being the most fulfilled man you can be.

Best of luck, guys!

Sincerely,

Ray Asher

P.S.

If you've found this book helpful in any way, a review on Amazon is greatly appreciated.

This means a lot to me, and I'll be extremely grateful.

Notes

[1] Jeffrey Hall (2014). "Flirting hard to detect". *The University of Kansas* (2014).

[2] Jeffrey Hall. "Flirtatious miscommunication." *The Academic Minute, A WAMC National Production, The University of Kansas* (2015)

More Books By Ray Asher

How to Talk to Women: Get Her to Like You & Want You With Effortless, Fun Conversation & Never Run Out of Anything to Say! How to Approach Women (Dating Advice for Men)

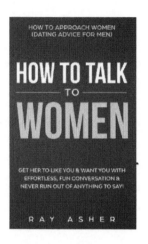

Discover How to Master the Art of Conversation, Effortlessly Engage and Deeply Connect with Women and Dramatically Improve Your Dating Life!

Tired of freezing up when in close proximity to an attractive woman you'd like to talk to?

Do you often run out of things to say when talking with a woman, only to watch her slowly lose interest?

If you want to stop all these in your life, then keep reading...

Learning how to effortlessly talk to women and getting them to open up to you is a skill that so few men have and can open up a world that you never knew existed.

Women are more likely to do you favors and even date you if you know how to approach and properly connect with them.

And it doesn't have to be difficult.

In this powerful guide, Ray Asher condenses his years of struggles, trials and errors and his eventual discovery of the secrets of deeply connecting with and attracting women using the power of conversation to help you bring the kind of women you desire into your life.

How to Talk to Women, **the only book you'll ever need to connect with women on a level she'd never experienced before.**

Here's a taste of what you'll discover inside *How to Talk to Women*:

- The 4 surefire conversational topics that are universally engaging to women

- 5 foolproof ways to have memorable conversations with women

- Simple tips to help you avoid turning off a woman with "mansplaining"

- An effective conversational template that you never run out of things to say

- 10 powerful listening tips to make a woman feel completely understood by you

- Effortless ways to get her to discuss sexual topics with you

- How to get past the small talk and get into a deep conversation with a woman

- 6 topics to avoid like the plague when in a conversation with a woman you're interested in

- How to tell an insanely good story that will have her hanging onto your every word

- Dating advice for men and pro tips to help you smoothly ask for her digits

And much, much more...

Whether you're completely clueless when it comes to women, or you're looking to sharpen your conversational skills with them, this guide will get you started on the way to a more charming, attractive version of yourself.

If you're ready to finally learn how to effortlessly talk to women without breaking a sweat, attract them and say goodbye to overwhelming shyness, now is the time.

How to Attract Women: Laugh Your Way to Effortless Dating & Relationship! Attracting Women By Knowing What They Want In A Man (Female Psychology for Understanding Them)

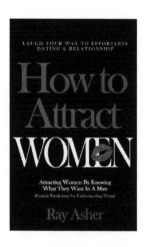

Do You Really, Really, REALLY Know What Women Want in a Man?

Are you single against your will?

Do you struggle when attracting women?

Do you feel that all the women you like are out of your league?

If you want to stop all these in your life, then keep reading...

Women don't care about that fancy pickup line you've found on the internet. They don't want to be put on a pedestal and blindly adored.

However, there are behaviors and skills that attract them like flowers attract bees – and they're often not the behaviors YOU think are sexy.

When Ray Asher started dating, he was unpopular with women. He tried being nice, being mean, playing games, wearing the latest fashions, memorizing sophisticated pickup lines... but nothing worked. Therefore, he began studying women to discover what they REALLY want in a man... and came to many surprising discoveries!

In *How to Attract Women*, you will discover the secrets to attract women from every city on the planet, create sharp sexual tension with the hottest women in the world, and build a relationship with the woman of your dreams!

Here's a taste of what you'll discover inside *How to Attract Women*:

- Women want a Good Guy, not a Nice Guy – learn the difference and show women how Good you are!

- Some of the behaviors you would call "masculine" actually scare women away – get to know and learn them!

- Women are attracted to certain skills and hobbies – learn exactly what skills are worth practicing and demonstrating

- Discover the one proven method to kill approach anxiety once and for all

- Train yourself to become confident – just read the step-by-step guide, put it into action and enjoy being confident around women!

- Understand how to text, talk and communicate in a seductive way

- Discover what women actually enjoy in bed and avoid mistakes that could ruin your relationship!

And much, much more...

Virgins became pickup artists...Heartbrokens to finding the love of their lives...friend-zoned to a player...this book will give you all the knowledge you need, all you have to do is EXECUTE.

Can you imagine your life with core confidence and abundance of women? If one man made it – then you can, too. Now it's your time.

Printed in Great Britain
by Amazon

29904212R00108